100 BEST
Chicken
RECIPES

pil

Publications International, Ltd.

Favorite Brand Name Recipes at www.fbnr.com

Pictured on the front cover: Chicken Tuscany *(page 32)*.

Pictured on the back cover *(clockwise from top left):* Homestyle Chicken Pot Pie *(page 8)*, Tangy Italian Chicken Sandwiches *(page 92)*, Mexicali Chicken Stew *(page 82)* and Spicy Mango Chicken *(page 128)*.

ISBN-13: 978-1-4127-2500-2
ISBN-10: 1-4127-2500-3

Library of Congress Control Number: 2007921118

Manufactured in China.

8 7 6 5 4 3 2 1

Microwave Cooking: Microwave ovens vary in wattage. Use the cooking times as guidelines and check for doneness before adding more time.

Preparation/Cooking Times: Preparation times are based on the approximate amount of time required to assemble the recipe before cooking, baking, chilling or serving. These times include preparation steps such as measuring, chopping and mixing. The fact that some preparations and cooking can be done simultaneously is taken into account. Preparation of optional ingredients and serving suggestions is not included.

Contents

Ultimate Classics   4

Comforting Casseroles   26

Sizzling Skillet Dinners   50

Savory Soups & Stews   70

Sandwiches & Salads   92

Hot Off The Grill   114

Quick-Fixin' Chicken   136

Acknowledgments   152

Index   153

Ultimate

CLASSICS

Chicken & Biscuits

¼ cup butter or margarine
4 boneless skinless chicken breasts (about 1¼ pounds),
    cut into ½-inch pieces
½ cup chopped onion
½ teaspoon dried thyme
½ teaspoon paprika
¼ teaspoon black pepper
1 can (about 14 ounces) chicken broth, divided
⅓ cup all-purpose flour
1 package (10 ounces) frozen peas and carrots
1 package (12 ounces) refrigerated biscuits

1. Preheat oven to 375°F. Melt butter in large skillet over medium heat. Add chicken, onion, thyme, paprika and pepper. Cook 5 minutes or until chicken is browned.

2. Combine ¼ cup chicken broth with flour in small bowl; stir until smooth. Add remaining chicken broth to skillet; bring to a boil. Gradually add flour mixture, stirring constantly to prevent lumps from forming. Simmer 5 minutes. Add peas and carrots; cook 2 minutes.

3. Transfer to 1½-quart casserole; top with biscuits. Bake 25 to 30 minutes or until biscuits are golden brown.

Makes 4 to 6 servings

Chicken & Biscuits

Chicken Fajitas

1 tablespoon vegetable oil
1 large green bell pepper, thinly sliced
1 large red bell pepper, thinly sliced
1 large onion, thinly sliced
1 clove garlic, minced
4 boneless skinless chicken breasts (about 1 pound), cut into strips
½ teaspoon dried oregano
2 tablespoons dry white wine or water
 Salt and black pepper
8 (8-inch) flour tortillas
 Guacamole (optional)

1. Preheat oven to 350°F. Heat oil in large skillet over medium-high heat. Add bell peppers, onion and garlic. Cook 3 to 4 minutes or until crisp-tender, stirring occasionally. Remove vegetables with slotted spoon; set aside.

2. Add chicken and oregano to skillet. Cook 4 minutes or until chicken is no longer pink in center, stirring occasionally.

3. Return vegetables to skillet. Add wine. Season with salt and black pepper; cover. Continue cooking 2 minutes or until thoroughly heated.

4. Meanwhile, stack tortillas and wrap in foil. Heat tortillas in oven 10 minutes or until warm. Fill tortillas with chicken mixture; serve with guacamole, if desired. *Makes 4 servings*

Chicken Fajitas

Homestyle Chicken Pot Pie

2 tablespoons butter or margarine, divided
1 pound boneless skinless chicken breasts, cut into 1-inch pieces
½ teaspoon salt
½ teaspoon dried thyme
¼ teaspoon black pepper
1 package (16 ounces) frozen mixed vegetables (such as potatoes, peas and carrots), thawed and drained
1 can (10¾ ounces) condensed cream of chicken or mushroom soup, undiluted
⅓ cup dry white wine or milk
1 refrigerated pie crust (½ of 15-ounce package), at room temperature

1. Preheat oven to 425°F. Melt 1 tablespoon butter in medium broilerproof skillet over medium-high heat. Add chicken; sprinkle with salt, thyme and pepper. Cook 1 minute, stirring frequently.

2. Reduce heat to medium-low. Stir in vegetables, soup and wine; simmer 5 minutes.

3. While soup mixture is simmering, unwrap pie crust. Using small cookie cutter, make 4 decorative cut-outs from pastry to allow steam to escape.

4. Remove chicken mixture from heat; top with pie crust. Melt remaining tablespoon butter. Brush pie crust with 2 teaspoons melted butter. Arrange cut-outs attractively over crust, if desired. Brush cut-outs with remaining 1 teaspoon melted butter. Bake 12 minutes.

5. Turn oven to broil; broil 4 to 5 inches from heat source 2 minutes or until crust is golden brown and chicken mixture is bubbly.

Makes 4 to 5 servings

Note: If you skin and debone your own chicken breasts, be sure to reserve both the bones and skin. Let these scraps collect in a plastic bag in your freezer and soon you'll have enough to make flavorful homemade chicken stock.

Homestyle Chicken Pot Pie

Spanish Rice & Chicken Skillet

1 tablespoon oil
4 chicken drumsticks (about 1 pound)
1 onion, chopped
½ medium green bell pepper, chopped
½ medium red bell pepper, chopped
1 package (about 4 ounces) Spanish rice mix
1 can (about 14 ounces) diced tomatoes
1¼ cups chicken broth

1. Heat oil in medium skillet over high heat until hot. Add chicken; cook 5 minutes or until lightly browned on all sides. Add onion and bell peppers; cook and stir 2 minutes.

2. Stir in rice mix, tomatoes and broth. Bring to a boil. Cover and simmer over low heat 15 minutes or until rice is tender and liquid is absorbed. Remove from heat and let stand, covered, 5 minutes.

Makes 4 servings

Ranch Crispy Chicken

¼ cup unseasoned dry bread crumbs or cornflake crumbs
1 packet (1 ounce) HIDDEN VALLEY® Original Ranch® Salad
    Dressing & Seasoning Mix
6 bone-in chicken pieces

Combine bread crumbs and salad dressing & seasoning mix in a gallon-size plastic food storage bag. Add chicken pieces; seal bag. Shake to coat chicken. Bake chicken on ungreased baking pan at 375°F for 50 minutes or until no longer pink in center and juices run clear.

Makes 4 to 6 servings

Chicken Curry

½ cup uncooked white rice
1 tablespoon butter or margarine
1 clove garlic, minced
1 teaspoon curry powder
¼ teaspoon ground ginger
2 boneless skinless chicken breasts, cut into ¾-inch cubes
1 small onion, thinly sliced
1 cup coarsely chopped apple, divided
3 tablespoons raisins
¼ cup water
1 teaspoon chicken bouillon granules
¼ cup plain fat-free yogurt
2 teaspoons all-purpose flour
   Green onion slices (optional)

1. Cook rice according to package directions.

2. Meanwhile, heat butter, garlic, curry powder and ginger in medium skillet over medium heat. Add chicken; cook and stir 2 minutes. Add onion, ¾ cup chopped apple and raisins; cook and stir 3 minutes. Stir in water and chicken bouillon. Reduce heat to low; cover and simmer 2 minutes.

3. Combine yogurt and flour in small bowl. Stir several tablespoons liquid from skillet into yogurt mixture. Stir yogurt mixture back into skillet. Cook and stir just until mixture starts to boil.

4. Serve chicken curry over rice; garnish with remaining ¼ cup chopped apple. Sprinkle with green onion slices, if desired.

Makes 2 servings

Prep and Cook Time: 28 minutes

Apple Pecan Chicken Roll-Ups

½ cup apple juice
½ cup **UNCLE BEN'S®** Instant Brown Rice
½ cup finely chopped unpeeled apple
¼ cup chopped pecans
3 tablespoons sliced green onions
4 boneless, skinless chicken breasts (about 1 pound)
1 tablespoon vegetable oil

1. Heat oven to 400°F. In small saucepan, bring apple juice to a boil. Add rice; cover. Reduce heat and simmer 8 to 10 minutes or until liquid is absorbed. Stir in apple, pecans and green onions. Remove from heat.

2. Flatten each chicken breast to about ¼-inch thickness by pounding between two pieces of waxed paper. Place ¼ of rice mixture on each chicken breast. Roll up, tucking in edges. Secure with toothpicks.

3. Heat oil in medium skillet over medium-high heat. Add chicken and cook 4 to 5 minutes or until lightly browned; place in shallow baking pan. Bake 20 to 25 minutes or until chicken is no longer pink in center. *Makes 4 servings*

Note: For this recipe, choose an apple variety that will retain its shape when cooked, such as Granny Smith, Golden Delicious or Jonathan.

Apple Pecan Chicken Roll-Up

Chicken and Pasta Primavera

1 tablespoon margarine or butter
¾ pound boneless, skinless chicken breasts, cut into thin strips
2 cloves garlic, finely chopped
1 cup water
½ cup dry white wine or water
1 package KNORR® Recipe Classics™ Spring Vegetable Soup, Dip
    and Recipe Mix
½ teaspoon freshly ground pepper
8 ounces linguine, cooked and drained
    Grated Parmesan cheese (optional)

• In large skillet, melt margarine over medium-high heat; cook chicken and garlic, stirring frequently, 5 minutes. Stir in water, wine, recipe mix and pepper. Bring to a boil over high heat, stirring constantly. Reduce heat to low; simmer 5 minutes or until chicken is no longer pink.

• Toss with pasta. Serve, if desired, with cheese.   *Makes 6 servings*

Prep Time: 20 minutes
Cook Time: 12 minutes

Crispy Baked Chicken

8 ounces (1 cup) French onion dip
½ cup milk
1 cup cornflake crumbs
½ cup wheat germ
6 skinless chicken breasts or thighs (about 1½ pounds)

Preheat oven to 350°F. Lightly grease shallow baking pan. Place dip in shallow bowl; stir until smooth. Add milk, 1 tablespoon at a time, until pourable consistency is reached. Combine cornflake crumbs and wheat germ on plate. Dip chicken pieces in milk mixture, then roll in cornflake mixture. Place chicken in single layer in prepared pan. Bake 45 to 50 minutes or until juices run clear and chicken is no longer pink near bone.   *Makes 6 servings*

Chicken and Pasta Primavera

Southern-Style Chicken and Greens

  1 teaspoon salt
  1 teaspoon paprika
  ½ teaspoon black pepper
3½ pounds chicken pieces
  4 thick slices smoked bacon (4 ounces), cut crosswise into ¼-inch
      strips
  1 cup uncooked rice
  1 can (about 14 ounces) stewed tomatoes
1¼ cups chicken broth
  2 cups packed stemmed and coarsely chopped fresh collard
      or mustard greens or kale (3 to 4 ounces)

1. Preheat oven to 350°F.

2. Combine salt, paprika and pepper in small bowl. Sprinkle meaty side of chicken pieces with salt mixture; set aside.

3. Place bacon in ovenproof Dutch oven; cook over medium heat until crisp. Remove from Dutch oven; drain on paper towels. Reserve drippings.

4. Heat drippings in Dutch oven over medium-high heat until hot. Arrange chicken in single layer in Dutch oven and cook 3 minutes per side or until chicken is browned. Transfer to plate; set aside. Repeat with remaining pieces. Reserve 1 tablespoon drippings in Dutch oven.

5. Add rice to drippings; cook and stir 1 minute. Add tomatoes, broth, collard greens and half of bacon; bring to a boil over high heat. Remove from heat; arrange chicken over rice mixture.

6. Bake, covered, about 40 minutes or until chicken pieces are no longer pink in center and most of liquid is absorbed. Let stand 5 minutes before serving. Transfer to serving platter; sprinkle with remaining bacon.   *Makes 4 to 6 servings*

Serving Suggestion: Serve with corn bread or corn muffins.

Southern-Style Chicken and Greens

Hidden Valley® Fried Chicken

1 broiler-fryer chicken, cut up (2 to 2½ pounds)
1 cup prepared HIDDEN VALLEY® The Original Ranch®
   Salad Dressing
¾ cup all-purpose flour
1 teaspoon salt
½ teaspoon freshly ground black pepper
   Vegetable oil

Place chicken pieces in shallow baking dish; pour salad dressing over chicken. Cover; refrigerate at least 8 hours. Remove chicken. Shake off excess marinade; discard marinade. Preheat oven to 350°F. On plate, mix flour, salt and pepper; roll chicken in seasoned flour. Heat ½ inch oil in large skillet until small cube of bread dropped into oil browns in 60 seconds or until oil is 375°F. Fry chicken until golden, 5 to 7 minutes on each side; transfer to baking pan. Bake until chicken is is no longer pink and juices run clear, about 30 minutes. Serve with corn muffins, if desired.   *Makes 4 main-dish servings*

tip *It's very important to heat the oil to the proper temperature when frying foods. If the oil isn't hot enough, the chicken will absorb fat and be greasy; if the oil is too hot, the chicken will burn. Use a deep-fat thermometer to obtain the most accurate temperature of the oil.*

Chicken Fricassee

3 pounds bone-in chicken pieces
  All-purpose flour
  Nonstick cooking spray
3 cups chicken broth
1 bay leaf
1 pound baby carrots
1 medium onion, cut into wedges
1 tablespoon butter or margarine
3 tablespoons all-purpose flour
¾ cup milk
1 tablespoon lemon juice
3 tablespoons minced fresh dill *or* 2 teaspoons dried dill weed
1 teaspoon sugar
½ teaspoon salt
6 cups hot cooked noodles

1. Coat chicken pieces very lightly with flour. Spray large skillet with cooking spray; heat over medium heat. Cook chicken 10 to 15 minutes or until browned on all sides. Drain fat from skillet.

2. Add chicken broth and bay leaf to skillet; bring to a boil. Reduce heat to low and simmer, covered, about 40 minutes or until chicken is cooked through (170°F for breast meat, 180°F for dark meat). Add carrots and onion during last 20 minutes of cooking time.

3. With slotted spoon, transfer chicken and vegetables to platter; keep warm. Bring broth to a boil; boil until reduced to 1 cup. Remove and discard bay leaf.

4. Melt butter in small saucepan over low heat; stir in 3 tablespoons flour. Cook and stir 1 to 2 minutes. Stir in broth, milk and lemon juice; bring to a boil. Boil until thickened, stirring constantly. Stir in dill, sugar and salt.

5. Serve chicken over noodles; top with sauce.   *Makes 6 servings*

Southwestern Chicken and Potato Hash

2 cups diced peeled potatoes
2 cups diced cooked chicken breast
1 medium onion, chopped
½ cup chopped green or red bell pepper
½ teaspoon salt
½ teaspoon chili powder
¼ teaspoon black pepper
1 egg white
1 tablespoon olive oil, divided
   Purchased or homemade corn bread (prepared in 8- or 9-inch
      square pan)
6 tablespoons salsa

1. Cover potatoes with water in small saucepan; bring to a boil.
Reduce heat and simmer 5 minutes or until just tender. Drain.

2. Combine potatoes, chicken, onion, bell pepper, salt, chili powder
and black pepper in large bowl; stir in egg white until well blended.

3. Heat oil in large nonstick skillet over medium heat. Add chicken
mixture; cook 6 to 8 minutes on each side or until brown and crisp.

4. Cut corn bread into 6 pieces; cut pieces in half horizontally. Place
bottom halves on plates. Spoon hash over corn bread; top with
remaining corn bread halves and salsa.   *Makes 6 servings*

*Southwestern Chicken and
Potato Hash*

Classic Chicken Parmesan

6 boneless, skinless chicken breasts, pounded thin (about
    1½ pounds)
2 eggs, slightly beaten
1 cup Italian seasoned dry bread crumbs
2 tablespoons BERTOLLI® Olive Oil
1 jar (1 pound 10 ounces) RAGÚ® Old World Style® Pasta Sauce
1 cup shredded mozzarella cheese (about 4 ounces)

Preheat oven to 375°F. Dip chicken in eggs, then bread crumbs,
coating well.

In 12-inch skillet, heat oil over medium-high heat and brown chicken;
drain on paper towels.

In 11×7-inch baking dish, evenly spread 1 cup Pasta Sauce. Arrange
chicken in dish, then top with remaining sauce. Sprinkle with
mozzarella cheese and, if desired, grated Parmesan cheese. Bake,
uncovered, 25 minutes or until chicken is no longer pink.

Makes 6 servings

tip
*To pound chicken, place a boneless skinless breast between
2 sheets of waxed paper. Use a rolling pin to press down and
out from the center to flatten.*

Monterey Chicken and Rice Quiche

4 boneless, skinless chicken tenderloins, cut into 1-inch pieces
1¾ cups water
1 box UNCLE BEN'S® COUNTRY INN® Chicken & Vegetable Rice
1 cup frozen mixed vegetables
1 (9-inch) deep-dish ready-to-use frozen pie crust
3 eggs
½ cup milk
½ cup (2 ounces) shredded Monterey Jack cheese

1. Heat oven to 400°F.

2. In large skillet, combine chicken, water, rice, contents of seasoning packet and frozen vegetables. Bring to a boil. Cover; reduce heat and simmer 10 minutes. Spoon mixture into pie crust.

3. In small bowl, beat eggs and milk. Pour over rice mixture in pie crust; top with cheese. Bake 30 to 35 minutes or until knife inserted into center comes out clean. *Makes 6 servings*

Serving Suggestion: A fresh fruit compote of orange sections and green grapes or blueberries is the perfect accompaniment to this delicious quiche.

Garlic 'n Lemon Roast Chicken

1 small onion, finely chopped
1 envelope LIPTON® RECIPE SECRETS® Savory Herb with Garlic
   Soup Mix
2 tablespoons olive or vegetable oil
2 tablespoons lemon juice
1 (3½-pound) roasting chicken

1. In large plastic bag or bowl, combine onion and soup mix blended with oil and lemon juice; add chicken. Close bag and shake, or toss in bowl, until chicken is evenly coated. Cover and marinate in refrigerator 2 hours, turning occasionally.

2. Preheat oven to 350°F. Arrange chicken, breast side up, with marinade, in 13×9-inch baking or roasting pan. Discard bag.

3. Bake uncovered, basting occasionally, 1 hour and 20 minutes or until meat thermometer reaches 180°F. (Insert meat thermometer into thickest part of thigh between breast and thigh; make sure tip does not touch bone.) *Makes 4 servings*

tip *Be sure to let the chicken rest at least 10 minutes after it's done cooking before you begin carving. This allows the juices to redistribute throughout the meat, resulting in a juicier chicken that is easier to carve. Cover the chicken loosely with foil during this time to keep it warm.*

Garlic 'n Lemon Roast Chicken

Comforting
CASSEROLES

Broccoli, Chicken and Rice Casserole

1 box UNCLE BEN'S CHEF'S RECIPE™ Broccoli Rice
   Au Gratin Supreme
2 cups boiling water
4 boneless, skinless chicken breasts (about 1 pound)
¼ teaspoon garlic powder
2 cups frozen broccoli
1 cup (4 ounces) shredded reduced-fat Cheddar cheese

1. Heat oven to 425°F. In 13×9-inch baking pan, combine rice and contents of seasoning packet. Add boiling water; mix well. Add chicken; sprinkle with garlic powder. Cover and bake 30 minutes.

2. Add broccoli and cheese; continue to bake, covered, 8 to 10 minutes or until chicken is no longer pink in center.

Makes 4 servings

Broccoli, Chicken and Rice Casserole

Barbecue Chicken with Corn Bread Topper

Nonstick cooking spray
1½ pounds boneless skinless chicken breasts and thighs, cut
  into ¾-inch cubes
1 can (about 15 ounces) red beans, rinsed and drained
1 cup chopped green bell pepper
1 can (8 ounces) tomato sauce
½ cup barbecue sauce
1 package (6 ounces) corn bread mix, plus ingredients to
  prepare mix

1. Spray large nonstick skillet with cooking spray. Heat over medium heat. Add chicken; cook and stir 5 minutes or until cooked through.

2. Combine chicken, beans, bell pepper, tomato sauce and barbecue sauce in 8-inch microwavable ovenproof dish.

3. Preheat oven to 375°F. Loosely cover chicken mixture with plastic wrap or waxed paper. Microwave on MEDIUM-HIGH (70%) 8 minutes or until heated through, stirring after 4 minutes.

4. While chicken mixture is heating, prepare corn bread mix according to package directions. Spoon batter over chicken mixture. Bake 15 to 18 minutes or until toothpick inserted into center of corn bread layer comes out clean. *Makes 8 servings*

Barbecue Chicken with
Corn Bread Topper

Mini Chicken Pot Pies

1 package (about 16 ounces) refrigerated reduced-fat buttermilk
    biscuits
1½ cups milk
1 package (1.8 ounces) white sauce mix
2 cups cut-up cooked chicken
1 cup frozen assorted vegetables, partially thawed
2 cups shredded Cheddar cheese
2 cups *French's®* French Fried Onions

1. Preheat oven to 400°F. Separate biscuits; press into 8 (8-ounce) custard cups, pressing up sides to form crust.

2. Whisk milk and sauce mix in medium saucepan. Bring to a boil over medium-high heat. Reduce heat to medium-low; simmer 1 minute, whisking constantly, until thickened. Stir in chicken and vegetables.

3. Spoon about ⅓ cup chicken mixture into each crust. Place cups on baking sheet. Bake 15 minutes or until golden brown. Top each with cheese and French Fried Onions. Bake 3 minutes or until golden. To serve, remove from cups and transfer to serving plates.

Makes 8 servings

Prep Time: 15 minutes
Cook Time: about 20 minutes

Herbed Chicken & Vegetables

2 medium all-purpose potatoes, thinly sliced (about 1 pound)
2 medium carrots, sliced
4 bone-in chicken pieces (about 2 pounds)
1 envelope LIPTON® RECIPE SECRETS® Savory Herb with Garlic
    Soup Mix
⅓ cup water
1 tablespoon olive or vegetable oil

1. Preheat oven to 425°F. In broiler pan, without the rack, place potatoes and carrots; arrange chicken on top. Pour soup mix blended with water and oil over chicken and vegetables.

2. Bake, uncovered, 40 minutes or until chicken is no longer pink and vegetables are tender. *Makes 4 servings*

Slow Cooker Method: Place all ingredients in slow cooker, arranging chicken on top; cover. Cook on LOW 6 to 8 hours or HIGH 4 hours.

Prep Time: 10 minutes
Cook Time: 40 minutes

> **tip** *If you have leftovers, don't leave them sitting out at room temperature for more than 2 hours. Cooked chicken should be refrigerated promptly to prevent the growth of harmful bacteria.*

Chicken Tuscany

6 medium red potatoes, scrubbed and sliced ⅛ inch thick
12 ounces shiitake, cremini, chanterelle and/or button mushrooms, sliced
4 tablespoons olive oil, divided
4 tablespoons grated Parmesan cheese, divided
3 teaspoons minced garlic, divided
3 teaspoons minced fresh rosemary leaves *or* 1½ teaspoons dried rosemary, divided
  Salt and ground pepper
1 package (about 3 pounds) PERDUE® fresh skinless Pick of the Chicken

Preheat oven to 425°F. Pat potatoes dry with paper towels. Toss potatoes and mushrooms with 2½ tablespoons oil, 2 tablespoons cheese, 2 teaspoons garlic, 2 teaspoons fresh rosemary, ½ teaspoon salt and ¼ teaspoon pepper. In 13×9-inch baking dish, arrange potatoes in one layer; top with remaining 2 tablespoons cheese. Bake 15 minutes or until potatoes are lightly browned; set aside.

Meanwhile, in large nonstick skillet over medium heat, heat remaining 1½ tablespoons oil. Add chicken pieces. Season lightly with salt and pepper; sprinkle with remaining fresh rosemary and garlic. Cook chicken 5 to 6 minutes on each side or until browned. (Do not crowd pan; if necessary, brown chicken in 2 batches.)

Arrange chicken on top of potato mixture in baking dish; drizzle with any remaining oil from skillet and return to oven. Bake 20 to 25 minutes longer or until chicken is no longer pink in center. Serve chicken, potatoes and mushrooms with green salad, if desired.

Makes 6 servings

Chicken Tuscany

Comforting Casseroles

Chicken Normandy Style

2 tablespoons butter, divided
3 cups peeled and thinly sliced sweet apples, such as Fuji or
    Braeburn (about 3 apples)
1 pound ground chicken
¼ cup apple brandy or apple juice
1 can (10¾ ounces) cream of chicken soup, undiluted
¼ cup finely chopped green onions, green part only
2 teaspoons minced fresh sage *or* ½ teaspoon dried sage
¼ teaspoon black pepper
1 package (12 ounces) egg noodles, cooked and drained

1. Preheat oven to 350°F.

2. Melt 1 tablespoon butter in 12-inch nonstick skillet. Add apple slices; cook and stir over medium heat 7 to 10 minutes or until tender. Remove apple slices from skillet; set aside.

3. Add ground chicken to same skillet; cook and stir over medium heat until cooked through, breaking up with spoon. Stir in apple brandy and cook 2 minutes. Stir in soup, green onions, sage, pepper and reserved apple slices; simmer 5 minutes.

4. Toss noodles with remaining 1 tablespoon butter. Spoon into well-greased 9-inch square pan. Top with chicken mixture. Bake 15 minutes or until hot. *Makes 4 servings*

Note: Substitute ground turkey, tofu crumbles or ground pork for chicken, if desired.

Oven-Baked Chicken Parmesan

4 boneless, skinless chicken breasts (about 1¼ pounds)
1 egg, slightly beaten
¾ cup Italian seasoned dry bread crumbs
1 jar (26 to 28 ounces) RAGÚ® Old World Style® Pasta Sauce
1 cup shredded mozzarella cheese (about 4 ounces)

1. Preheat oven to 400°F. Dip chicken in egg, then bread crumbs, coating well.

2. In 13×9-inch glass baking dish, arrange chicken. Bake, uncovered, 20 minutes.

3. Pour Pasta Sauce over chicken, then top with cheese. Bake an additional 10 minutes or until chicken is no longer pink. Serve, if desired, with hot cooked pasta. *Makes 4 servings*

Prep Time: 10 minutes
Cook Time: 30 minutes

tip *Raw poultry should be stored in the coldest part of the refrigerator as soon as you get home from the supermarket. It can be stored up to 2 days in the refrigerator or up to 6 months in the freezer. When freezing poultry, remove it from its original packaging and seal it airtight in a freezer food storage bag or foil. Wrap it as tightly as possible to prevent ice crystals from forming and causing "freezer burn."*

Mexican Lasagna

2 tablespoons vegetable oil
4 boneless skinless chicken breasts (about 1 pound), cut into ½-inch pieces
2 teaspoons chili powder
1 teaspoon ground cumin
1 can (about 14 ounces) diced tomatoes with garlic, drained
1 can (8 ounces) tomato sauce
1 teaspoon hot pepper sauce (optional)
1 cup part-skim ricotta cheese
1 can (4 ounces) diced mild green chiles
¼ cup chopped fresh cilantro, divided
12 (6-inch) corn tortillas
1 cup (4 ounces) shredded Cheddar cheese

1. Preheat oven to 375°F.

2. Heat oil in large skillet over medium heat. Add chicken, chili powder and cumin. Cook 4 minutes or until tender, stirring occasionally. Stir in diced tomatoes, tomato sauce and hot pepper sauce, if desired; bring to a boil. Reduce heat; simmer 2 minutes.

3. Combine ricotta cheese, chiles and 2 tablespoons cilantro in small bowl; mix until well blended.

4. Spoon half of chicken mixture into bottom of 12×8-inch baking dish. Top with 6 tortillas, ricotta cheese mixture, remaining 6 tortillas, remaining chicken mixture, Cheddar cheese and remaining 2 tablespoons cilantro. Bake 25 minutes or until heated through.

Makes 6 to 8 servings

Mexican Lasagna

Cheesy Garlic Chicken

4 boneless, skinless chicken breasts (about 1¼ pounds)
1 medium tomato, coarsely chopped
1 envelope LIPTON® RECIPE SECRETS® Savory Herb with Garlic
    Soup Mix
⅓ cup water
1 tablespoon olive or vegetable oil
1 cup shredded mozzarella cheese (about 4 ounces)
1 tablespoon grated Parmesan cheese

1. Preheat oven to 400°F. In 13×9-inch baking dish, arrange chicken; top with tomato.

2. Pour soup mix blended with water and oil over chicken.

3. Bake, uncovered, 20 minutes. Top with cheeses and bake 5 minutes or until cheese is melted and chicken is no longer pink. Serve, if desired, with crusty Italian bread.   *Makes 4 servings*

Recipe Tip: Turn leftover Cheesy Garlic Chicken into a quick and delicious lunch or dinner. Simply heat and serve on hot store-bought garlic bread.

Prep Time: 5 minutes
Cook Time: 25 minutes

Cheesy Garlic Chicken

Chicken and Black Bean Enchiladas

2 jars (16 ounces each) mild picante sauce
¼ cup chopped fresh cilantro
2 tablespoons chili powder
1 teaspoon ground cumin
2 cups (10 ounces) chopped cooked chicken
1 can (15 ounces) black beans, rinsed and drained
1⅓ cups *French's®* French Fried Onions, divided
1 package (about 10 ounces) flour tortillas (7 inches)
1 cup (4 ounces) shredded Monterey Jack cheese with jalapeño peppers

Preheat oven to 350°F. Grease 15×10-inch jelly-roll baking pan. Combine picante sauce, cilantro, chili powder and cumin in large saucepan. Bring to a boil. Reduce heat to low; simmer 5 minutes.

Combine 1½ cups sauce mixture, chicken, beans and ⅔ *cup* French Fried Onions in medium bowl. Spoon a scant ½ cup filling over bottom third of each tortilla. Roll up tortillas, enclosing filling, and arrange, seam side down, in a single layer in bottom of prepared baking pan. Spoon remaining sauce evenly over tortillas.

Bake, uncovered, 20 minutes or until heated through. Sprinkle with remaining ⅔ *cup* onions and cheese. Bake 5 minutes or until cheese is melted and onions are golden. Serve immediately.

Makes 5 to 6 servings (4 cups sauce, 4½ cups filling)

Hint: This is a great make-ahead party dish.

Prep Time: 45 minutes
Cook Time: 25 minutes

Chicken Rice Casserole

4 tablespoons butter, divided
4 boneless skinless chicken breasts
1½ cups uncooked converted rice
6 ounces HILLSHIRE FARM® Lit'l Smokies
1 can (about 14 ounces) cream of chicken soup
1 can (about 14 ounces) cream of celery soup
1 cup sliced mushrooms
½ cup dry sherry
  Bread crumbs
  Cheddar cheese
  Slivered almonds

Preheat oven to 275°F.

Melt 2 tablespoons butter in large skillet over medium-high heat. Add chicken; sauté until cooked through, about 7 minutes on each side. Remove chicken and cut into bite-size pieces.

Place rice on bottom of medium casserole; add chicken, Lit'l Smokies, soups, ¾ cup water, mushrooms, sherry and remaining 2 tablespoons butter. Bake, covered, 2½ hours. Top casserole with bread crumbs, cheese and almonds. Broil until golden brown and cheese is melted.

Makes 6 to 8 servings

Note: Be sure to avoid overcooking—a major pitfall of casseroles destined for the freezer. One simple way to prevent this is to undercook any pasta or rice used in the recipe; it will cook through when the casserole is reheated.

Indian Spiced Chicken with Wild Rice

½ teaspoon salt
½ teaspoon ground cumin
½ teaspoon black pepper
¼ teaspoon ground cinnamon
¼ teaspoon ground turmeric
4 boneless skinless chicken breasts (about 1 pound)
2 tablespoons olive oil
2 carrots, sliced
1 red bell pepper, chopped
1 stalk celery, chopped
2 cloves garlic, minced
1 package (6 ounces) long grain and wild rice mix
2 cups reduced-sodium chicken broth
1 cup raisins
¼ cup sliced almonds

1. Combine salt, cumin, black pepper, cinnamon and turmeric in small bowl. Rub spice mixture on both sides of chicken. Place chicken on plate; cover and refrigerate 30 minutes.

2. Preheat oven to 350°F. Spray 13×9-inch baking dish with nonstick cooking spray.

3. Heat oil in large skillet over medium-high heat. Add chicken; cook 2 minutes per side or until browned. Remove chicken; set aside.

4. Place carrots, bell pepper, celery and garlic in same skillet. Cook and stir 2 minutes. Add rice; cook 5 minutes, stirring frequently. Add seasoning packet from rice mix and broth; bring to a boil over high heat. Remove from heat; stir in raisins. Pour into prepared dish; place chicken on rice mixture. Sprinkle with almonds.

5. Cover tightly with foil and bake 35 minutes or until chicken is no longer pink in center and rice is tender.   *Makes 4 servings*

*Indian Spiced Chicken with
Wild Rice*

Chicken & Rice Bake

1 can (10¾ ounces) condensed cream of mushroom soup
1¾ cups water
1½ cups sliced mushrooms
¾ cup uncooked long-grain rice
1⅓ cups *French's®* French Fried Onions, divided
4 teaspoons *French's®* Worcestershire Sauce, divided
4 chicken breasts (about 2 pounds)
½ teaspoon paprika
½ teaspoon dried thyme

1. Preheat oven to 375°F. Combine soup, water, mushrooms, rice, ⅔ cup French Fried Onions and 2 teaspoons Worcestershire in 3-quart oblong baking dish. Arrange chicken over rice mixture. Brush chicken with remaining Worcestershire and sprinkle with paprika and thyme.

2. Bake, uncovered, 1 hour or until chicken is no longer pink in center. Top with remaining ⅔ *cup* onions. Bake 3 minutes or until onions are golden. *Makes 4 servings*

Note: Remove skin from chicken before baking, if desired.

Prep Time: 10 minutes
Cook Time: about 1 hour

Chicken & Rice Bake

Pizza Chicken Bake

3½ cups uncooked bow tie pasta
1 tablespoon vegetable oil
1 cup sliced mushrooms
1 jar (26 ounces) herb-flavored spaghetti sauce
1 teaspoon pizza seasoning blend
3 boneless skinless chicken breasts (about ¾ pound), quartered
1 cup (4 ounces) shredded mozzarella cheese

1. Preheat oven to 350°F. Spray 2-quart round casserole with nonstick cooking spray.

2. Cook pasta according to package directions until al dente. Drain and place in prepared dish.

3. Meanwhile, heat oil in large skillet over medium-high heat. Add mushrooms; cook and stir 2 minutes. Remove from heat. Stir in spaghetti sauce and pizza seasoning.

4. Pour half of spaghetti sauce mixture into casserole; stir until pasta is well coated. Arrange chicken on top of pasta. Pour remaining spaghetti sauce mixture evenly over chicken.

5. Bake, covered, 50 minutes or until chicken is no longer pink in center. Remove from oven; sprinkle with cheese. Cover and let stand 5 minutes before serving.   *Makes 4 servings*

Serving Suggestion: Serve this casserole with grated Parmesan cheese and red pepper flakes on the side.

Chicken–Asparagus Casserole

2 teaspoons vegetable oil
1 cup seeded and chopped green and/or red bell peppers
1 medium onion, chopped
2 cloves garlic, minced
1 can (10¾ ounces) condensed cream of asparagus soup, undiluted
1 container (8 ounces) ricotta cheese
2 cups (8 ounces) shredded Cheddar cheese, divided
2 eggs
1½ cups chopped cooked chicken
1 package (10 ounces) frozen chopped asparagus,* thawed and
    drained
8 ounces uncooked egg noodles, cooked
    Black pepper (optional)

Or, substitute ½ pound fresh asparagus cut into ½-inch pieces. Bring 6 cups water to a boil over high heat in large saucepan. Add fresh asparagus. Reduce heat to medium. Cover and cook 5 to 8 minutes or until crisp-tender. Drain.

1. Preheat oven to 350°F. Grease 13×9-inch casserole; set aside.

2. Heat oil in small skillet over medium heat. Add bell peppers, onion and garlic; cook and stir until vegetables are crisp-tender.

3. Mix soup, ricotta cheese, 1 cup Cheddar cheese and eggs in large bowl until well blended. Add bell pepper mixture, chicken, asparagus and noodles; mix well. Season with black pepper, if desired.

4. Spread mixture evenly in prepared casserole. Top with remaining 1 cup Cheddar cheese.

5. Bake 30 minutes or until center is set and cheese is bubbly. Let stand 5 minutes before serving. *Makes 12 servings*

Creamy Chicken and Pasta with Spinach

6 ounces uncooked egg noodles
1 tablespoon olive oil
¼ cup chopped onion
¼ cup chopped red bell pepper
1 package (10 ounces) frozen spinach, thawed and drained
2 boneless skinless chicken breasts (about ¾ pound), cooked and
    cut into 1-inch pieces
1 can (4 ounces) sliced mushrooms, drained
2 cups (8 ounces) shredded Swiss cheese
1 container (8 ounces) sour cream
¾ cup half-and-half
2 eggs, slightly beaten
½ teaspoon salt

1. Preheat oven to 350°F. Prepare egg noodles according to package directions; set aside.

2. Heat oil in large skillet over medium-high heat. Add onion and bell pepper; cook and stir 2 minutes or until onion is tender. Add spinach, chicken, mushrooms and cooked noodles; stir to combine.

3. Combine cheese, sour cream, half-and-half, eggs and salt in medium bowl; blend well. Add cheese mixture to chicken mixture; stir to combine.

4. Pour skillet mixture into 13×9-inch baking dish coated with nonstick cooking spray. Bake, covered, 30 to 35 minutes or until heated through. *Makes 8 servings*

*Creamy Chicken and Pasta
with Spinach*

Sizzling

SKILLET DINNERS

Tomato, Basil & Broccoli Chicken

4 boneless, skinless chicken breasts
Salt and black pepper (optional)
2 tablespoons margarine or butter
1 package (6.9 ounces) RICE-A-RONI® Chicken Flavor
1 teaspoon dried basil
2 cups broccoli florets
1 medium tomato, seeded, chopped
1 cup (4 ounces) shredded mozzarella cheese

1. Sprinkle chicken with salt and pepper, if desired.

2. In large skillet, melt margarine over medium-high heat. Add chicken; cook 2 minutes per side or until browned. Remove chicken from skillet reserving drippings. Keep warm.

3. In same skillet, sauté rice-vermicelli mix in reserved drippings over medium heat until vermicelli is golden brown. Stir in 2½ cups water, Special Seasonings and basil. Place chicken over rice mixture; bring to a boil over high heat.

4. Cover; reduce heat. Simmer 15 minutes. Top with broccoli and tomato. Cover; continue to simmer 5 minutes or until liquid is absorbed and chicken is no longer pink in center. Sprinkle with cheese. Cover; let stand a few minutes before serving. *Makes 4 servings*

Tomato, Basil & Broccoli Chicken

Chicken Sauté with Olive Sauce

1 tablespoon olive oil
4 boneless, skinless chicken breasts (about 1½ pounds)
¼ cup orange juice
2 tablespoons white wine vinegar
2 tablespoons sliced green olives
2 tablespoons chopped pimiento
2 tablespoons chopped fresh parsley
2 tablespoons sliced almonds
1 clove garlic, minced
1 tablespoon sliced black olives
1 large green bell pepper, sliced into rings
1 Roma tomato, sliced
3 cups hot cooked rice

Heat oil in large skillet over medium-high heat. Add chicken; cook
6 to 8 minutes on each side or until no longer pink in center. Remove
chicken; keep warm. Reduce heat to medium; add orange juice,
vinegar, green olives, pimiento, parsley, almonds, garlic and black
olives to skillet. Cook and stir 2 to 3 minutes. To serve, arrange pepper
and tomato over hot rice on serving platter. Top with chicken. Spoon
sauce mixture over top. *Makes 4 servings*

Favorite recipe from **USA Rice Federation**

Chicken and Linguine in Creamy Tomato Sauce

1 tablespoon olive or vegetable oil
1 pound boneless, skinless chicken breasts, cut into ½-inch strips
1 jar (26 to 28 ounces) RAGÚ® Old World Style® Pasta Sauce
2 cups water
8 ounces uncooked linguine or spaghetti
½ cup whipping or heavy cream
1 tablespoon fresh basil leaves, chopped *or* 1 teaspoon dried basil
   leaves, crushed

1. In 12-inch skillet, heat oil over medium heat and brown chicken. Remove chicken and set aside.

2. In same skillet, stir in Pasta Sauce and water. Bring to a boil over high heat. Stir in uncooked linguine and return to a boil. Reduce heat to low and simmer covered, stirring occasionally, 15 minutes or until linguine is tender.

3. Stir in cream and basil. Return chicken to skillet and cook 5 minutes or until chicken is no longer pink.   *Makes 4 servings*

Prep Time: 10 minutes
Cook Time: 30 minutes

Skillet Chicken Cacciatore

2 tablespoons olive or vegetable oil
1 cup sliced red onion
1 medium green bell pepper, cut into strips (about 1 cup)
2 cloves garlic, minced
1 pound (about 4) boneless, skinless chicken breasts
1 can (14.5 ounces) CONTADINA® Recipe Ready Diced Tomatoes
   with Italian Herbs, undrained
¼ cup dry white wine or chicken broth
½ teaspoon salt
¼ teaspoon ground black pepper
1 tablespoon chopped fresh basil *or* 1 teaspoon dried basil leaves,
   crushed

1. Heat oil in large skillet over medium-high heat. Add onion, bell pepper and garlic; sauté 1 minute.

2. Add chicken; cook 6 to 8 minutes or until chicken is no longer pink in center.

3. Add undrained tomatoes, wine, salt and black pepper. Simmer, uncovered, 5 minutes. Serve over hot cooked rice or pasta, if desired. Sprinkle with basil. *Makes 6 servings*

Skillet Chicken Cacciatore

Simmered Tuscan Chicken

2 tablespoons olive or vegetable oil
1 pound boneless, skinless chicken breasts, cut into 1-inch cubes
2 cloves garlic, finely chopped
4 medium potatoes, cut into ½-inch cubes (about 4 cups)
1 medium red bell pepper, cut into large pieces
1 jar (26 to 28 ounces) RAGÚ® Old World Style® Pasta Sauce
1 pound fresh or frozen cut green beans
1 teaspoon dried basil leaves, crushed
   Salt and ground black pepper to taste

In 12-inch skillet, heat oil over medium-high heat; cook chicken with garlic until chicken is no longer pink. Remove chicken from skillet.

In same skillet, add potatoes and bell pepper. Cook over medium heat, stirring occasionally, 5 minutes. Stir in remaining ingredients. Bring to a boil over high heat. Reduce heat to low and simmer covered, stirring occasionally, 35 minutes or until potatoes are tender. Return chicken to skillet and heat through.   *Makes 6 servings*

Chicken & Wild Rice Skillet Dinner

1 tablespoon butter or margarine
¼ pound boneless skinless chicken breast (about 1 breast), cut
   into strips
1 package (about 6 ounces) long grain and wild rice mix with
   seasoning
1¾ cups water
6 dried apricots, cut up

1. Melt butter in medium skillet over medium-high heat. Add chicken; cook and stir 3 to 5 minutes or until cooked through.

2. Add rice, seasoning mix, water and apricots to skillet; mix well. Bring mixture to a boil. Cover and reduce heat to low; simmer 25 minutes or until liquid is absorbed and rice is tender.

Makes 2 servings

56

Chicken Puttanesca-Style

2 tablespoons BERTOLLI® Olive Oil
1 (2½- to 3-pound) chicken, cut into pieces
1 medium onion, sliced
¼ cup balsamic vinegar
1 jar (1 pound 10 ounces) RAGÚ® Old World Style® Pasta Sauce
1 cup pitted ripe olives
1 tablespoon drained capers

In 12-inch skillet, heat oil over medium-high heat and brown chicken. Remove chicken and set aside; drain.

In same skillet, add onion and vinegar and cook over medium heat, stirring occasionally, 3 minutes. Stir in Pasta Sauce. Return chicken to skillet and simmer, covered, 25 minutes or until chicken is no longer pink. Stir in olives and capers; heat through. Serve, if desired, over hot cooked rice and garnish with chopped fresh parsley.   *Makes 4 servings*

Note: In general, the longer balsamic vinegar has been aged, the deeper and tastier the flavor.

Chicken Rustigo

4 boneless skinless chicken breasts
1 package (10 ounces) fresh mushrooms, sliced
¾ cup chicken broth
¼ cup dry red wine or water
3 tablespoons *French's*® Zesty Deli Mustard
2 plum tomatoes, coarsely chopped
1 can (14 ounces) artichoke hearts, drained and quartered
2 teaspoons cornstarch

1. Season chicken with salt and pepper. Heat *1 tablespoon oil* in large nonstick skillet over medium-high heat. Cook chicken 5 minutes or until browned on both sides. Remove and set aside.

2. Heat *1 tablespoon oil* in same skillet over medium-high heat. Add mushrooms. Cook and stir 5 minutes or until mushrooms are tender. Stir in broth, wine and mustard. Return chicken to skillet. Add tomatoes and artichoke hearts. Heat to boiling. Reduce heat to medium-low. Cook, covered, 10 minutes or until chicken is no longer pink in center.

3. Combine cornstarch and *1 tablespoon cold water* in small bowl. Stir into skillet. Heat to boiling. Cook, stirring, over high heat about 1 minute or until sauce thickens. Serve with hot cooked orzo pasta, if desired.   *Makes 4 servings*

Prep Time: 10 minutes
Cook Time: 21 minutes

Chicken Rustigo

Coq au Vin & Pasta

4 large or 8 small chicken thighs (2 to 2½ pounds), trimmed of
   excess fat
2 teaspoons rotisserie or herb chicken seasoning*
1 tablespoon margarine or butter
3 cups (8 ounces) halved or quartered mushrooms
1 medium onion, coarsely chopped
½ cup dry white wine or vermouth
1 (4.9-ounce) package PASTA RONI® Homestyle Chicken Flavor
½ cup sliced green onions

*1 teaspoon paprika and 1 teaspoon garlic salt may be substituted.

1. Sprinkle meaty side of chicken with rotisserie seasoning. In
large skillet over medium-high heat, melt margarine. Add chicken,
seasoned side down; cook 3 minutes. Reduce heat to medium-low;
turn chicken over.

2. Add mushrooms, onion and wine. Cover; simmer 15 to 18 minutes
or until chicken is no longer pink inside. Remove chicken from skillet;
set aside.

3. In same skillet, bring 1 cup water to a boil. Stir in pasta, green
onions and Special Seasonings. Place chicken over pasta. Reduce heat
to medium-low. Cover; gently boil 6 to 8 minutes or until pasta is
tender. Let stand 3 to 5 minutes before serving.   *Makes 4 servings*

Prep Time: 10 minutes
Cook Time: 30 minutes

Coq au Vin & Pasta

Harvest Apple Chicken & Rice

2 tablespoons margarine or butter, divided
4 boneless, skinless chicken breasts (about 1 pound)
1 (6.0-ounce) package RICE-A-RONI® Herb Roasted Chicken Flavor
1 cup apple juice
1 medium apple, chopped (about 1 cup)
1 cup sliced mushrooms
½ cup chopped onion
¼ cup dried cranberries or raisins

1. In large skillet over medium-high heat, melt 1 tablespoon margarine. Add chicken; cook 2 minutes on each side or until browned. Remove from skillet; set aside.

2. In same skillet over medium heat, sauté rice-vermicelli mix with remaining 1 tablespoon margarine until pasta is golden brown.

3. Slowly stir in 1¼ cups water, apple juice, apple, mushrooms, onion, cranberries and Special Seasonings; bring to a boil. Place chicken over rice. Reduce heat to medium-low. Cover; simmer 15 to 20 minutes or until chicken is no longer pink inside and rice is tender. Let stand 5 minutes before serving.   *Makes 4 servings*

Note: There's no need to peel the apple—the peel adds extra color and texture.

Prep Time: 10 minutes
Cook Time: 35 minutes

Harvest Apple Chicken & Rice

Orange Chicken Piccata

1 pound boneless skinless chicken breasts, pounded thin
2 tablespoons flour
½ cup orange juice
¼ cup _French's®_ Sweet & Tangy Honey Mustard
¼ cup orange marmalade
¼ teaspoon dried rosemary
1 orange, thinly sliced and quartered

1. Coat chicken with flour; shake off excess. Heat _1 tablespoon oil_ in nonstick skillet. Cook chicken 5 minutes or until browned.

2. Mix orange juice, mustard, marmalade and rosemary. Add to skillet. Bring to boiling. Simmer, uncovered, over medium-low heat for 5 minutes or until chicken is no longer pink in center and sauce thickens slightly.

3. Stir in orange pieces; heat through. Serve with rice, if desired.

Makes 4 servings

Prep Time: 5 minutes
Cook Time: 10 minutes

Orange Chicken Piccata

Tomato Chutney Chicken

4 boneless, skinless chicken breast halves
1 can (16 ounces) tomatoes with juice, cut up
1 cup peeled and chopped cooking apple
¼ cup chopped onion
¼ cup chopped green bell pepper
¼ cup golden raisins
2 tablespoons brown sugar
2 tablespoons lemon juice
1 teaspoon grated lemon peel
1 clove garlic, minced
½ teaspoon ground cinnamon
¼ teaspoon red pepper flakes
¼ teaspoon salt

In large skillet, place tomatoes with juice, apple, onion, green pepper, raisins, brown sugar, lemon juice, lemon peel, garlic, cinnamon and red pepper flakes; stir to mix. Cook, stirring, over medium-high heat until mixture boils. Sprinkle salt over chicken breasts. Place chicken over tomato mixture. Reduce heat to medium-low; cover and cook, stirring and turning frequently, about 15 minutes or until chicken is fork-tender. Arrange chicken on serving platter; spoon sauce over chicken.   *Makes 4 servings*

*Favorite recipe from **Delmarva Poultry Industry, Inc.***

Bistro Chicken Skillet

1 (2- to 2½-pound) whole chicken, cut into 8 pieces
2 teaspoons dried thyme
1 teaspoon salt
1 teaspoon paprika
½ teaspoon ground black pepper
2 tablespoons olive oil
8 large whole cloves garlic, peeled
¼ cup dry vermouth or water
2 tablespoons margarine or butter
1 (4.6-ounce) package PASTA RONI® Garlic & Olive Oil with
   Vermicelli
1½ cups fresh asparagus, cut into 1½-inch pieces or broccoli
   flowerets
1 cup sliced carrots

1. Sprinkle meaty side of chicken with thyme, salt, paprika and pepper. In large skillet over medium-high heat, heat oil. Add chicken, seasoned side down. Cook 5 minutes. Reduce heat to medium-low; turn chicken over. Add garlic. Cover; cook 20 to 25 minutes or until chicken is no longer pink inside.

2. Meanwhile, in medium saucepan, bring 1½ cups water, vermouth and margarine just to a boil. Stir in pasta, asparagus, carrots and Special Seasonings. Reduce heat to medium. Gently boil, uncovered, 10 minutes or until pasta is tender, stirring occasionally.

3. Remove chicken and garlic from skillet with slotted spoon. Skim off and discard fat from skillet juices. Serve chicken, garlic and reserved juices over pasta.   *Makes 4 servings*

Prep Time: 10 minutes
Cook Time: 35 minutes

Mediterranean Skillet Chicken

1 can (10¾ ounces) condensed reduced-fat tomato soup, undiluted
½ cup water
¼ cup golden raisins
1 can (2¼ ounces) sliced black olives, drained
2 cloves garlic, minced
¾ teaspoon dried basil
¾ teaspoon dried oregano
   Nonstick cooking spray
4 boneless skinless chicken breasts (about 1 pound), cut into strips
1 cup sliced zucchini
½ cup red or green bell pepper strips
3 cups hot cooked rice

1. Combine soup, water, raisins, olives, garlic, basil and oregano in medium bowl; set aside.

2. Spray large nonstick skillet with cooking spray. Add chicken; cook and stir over high heat until cooked through. Remove from skillet; set aside.

3. Add zucchini and bell pepper to skillet; cook and stir 2 to 3 minutes. Reduce heat to medium; stir in soup mixture. Return chicken to skillet and cook until mixture is heated through. Serve over rice.

Makes 4 servings

tip *Dark raisins and golden raisins come from the same grapes. Dark raisins get their dark color and shriveled appearance from being sun-dried for several weeks; golden raisins are treated with sulphur dioxide and artificial heat, leaving them lighter and plumper. If you don't have golden raisins for this recipe, dark raisins can be substituted.*

Mediterranean Skillet Chicken

Savory

SOUPS & STEWS

Country Chicken Chowder

2 tablespoons butter or margarine
1 pound chicken tenders, cut into ½-inch pieces
1 small onion, chopped
1 stalk celery, sliced
1 small carrot, sliced
1 can (10¾ ounces) cream of potato soup, undiluted
1 cup milk
1 cup frozen corn
½ teaspoon dried dill weed
   Salt and black pepper

1. Melt butter in large saucepan or Dutch oven over medium-high heat. Add chicken; cook and stir 5 minutes.

2. Add onion, celery and carrot; cook and stir 3 minutes. Stir in soup, milk, corn and dill; reduce heat to low. Cook about 8 minutes or until corn is tender and chowder is heated through. Add salt and pepper to taste. Garnish with croutons and fresh dill, if desired.   *Makes 4 servings*

Serving Suggestion: For a hearty winter meal, serve the chowder in hollowed-out toasted French rolls or small, round sourdough loaves.

Country Chicken Chowder

Tex-Mex Chicken & Rice Chili

1 package (6.8 ounces) RICE-A-RONI® Spanish Rice
2¾ cups water
2 cups chopped cooked chicken or turkey
1 can (15 to 16 ounces) kidney beans or pinto beans, rinsed and
   drained
1 can (about 14 ounces) tomatoes or stewed tomatoes
1 medium green bell pepper, cut into ½-inch pieces
1½ teaspoons chili powder
1 teaspoon ground cumin
½ cup (2 ounces) shredded Cheddar or Monterey Jack cheese
   (optional)
   Sour cream (optional)
   Chopped fresh cilantro (optional)

1. In 3-quart saucepan, combine rice-vermicelli mix, Special
Seasonings, water, chicken, beans, tomatoes, green bell pepper,
chili powder and cumin. Bring to a boil over high heat.

2. Reduce heat to low; simmer, uncovered, about 20 minutes or
until rice is tender, stirring occasionally.

3. Top with cheese, sour cream and cilantro, if desired.

Makes 4 servings

Tex-Mex Chicken & Rice Chili

72

Country Chicken Stew with Dumplings

1 tablespoon BERTOLLI® Olive Oil
1 whole chicken (3 to 3½ pounds), cut into serving pieces (with or without skin)
4 large carrots, cut into 2-inch pieces
3 ribs celery, cut into 1-inch pieces
1 large onion, cut into 1-inch wedges
1 envelope LIPTON® RECIPE SECRETS® Savory Herb with Garlic Soup Mix*
1½ cups water
½ cup apple juice
Parsley Dumplings (recipe follows), optional

*Also terrific with Lipton® Recipe Secrets® Golden Onion Soup Mix.

In 6-quart Dutch oven or heavy saucepot, heat oil over medium-high heat and brown half of the chicken; remove and set aside. Repeat with remaining chicken. Return chicken to Dutch oven. Stir in carrots, celery, onion and savory herb with garlic soup mix blended with water and apple juice. Bring to a boil over high heat. Reduce heat to low; simmer, covered, 25 minutes or until chicken is cooked through, juices run clear and vegetables are tender.

Meanwhile, prepare Parsley Dumplings. Drop 12 rounded tablespoonfuls of batter into simmering broth around chicken. Continue simmering, covered, 10 minutes or until toothpick inserted into centers of dumplings comes out clean. Season stew, if desired, with salt and black pepper.   *Makes about 6 servings*

Parsley Dumplings: In medium bowl, combine 1⅓ cups all-purpose flour, 2 teaspoons baking powder, 1 tablespoon chopped fresh parsley and ½ teaspoon salt; set aside. In measuring cup, blend ⅔ cup milk, 2 tablespoons melted butter or margarine and 1 egg. Stir milk mixture into flour mixture just until blended.

Variation: Add 1 pound quartered red potatoes to stew with carrots; eliminate dumplings.

Country Chicken Stew
with Dumplings

Chicken Tortilla Soup

2 large ripe avocados, halved and pitted
4 teaspoons TABASCO® brand Green Pepper Sauce, divided
½ teaspoon salt *or to taste*
3 (14½-ounce) cans chicken broth
3 boneless, skinless chicken breasts (about 1 pound)
2 tablespoons uncooked rice
1 large tomato, seeded and chopped
½ cup chopped onion
¼ cup finely chopped fresh cilantro
　Tortilla chips
½ cup (2 ounces) shredded Monterey Jack cheese

Scoop out avocado into medium bowl and mash with fork. Add 1½ teaspoons TABASCO® Green Pepper Sauce and salt; blend gently but thoroughly. Set aside.

Heat chicken broth to boiling in 4-quart saucepan. Add chicken breasts; reduce heat and cook until chicken is opaque. Remove chicken and cut into bite-size pieces. Add rice and cook about 15 minutes or until tender. Return chicken to saucepan. Just before serving, stir in tomato, onion, cilantro and remaining 2½ teaspoons TABASCO® Green Pepper Sauce.

To serve, break small handful of tortilla chips into bottom of each bowl. Ladle soup over tortilla chips. Top with cheese and 1 rounded tablespoon avocado mixture. Serve immediately with additional TABASCO® Green Pepper Sauce, if desired.　　*Makes 8 servings*

Chicken Tortilla Soup

Black and White Chili

Nonstick cooking spray
1 pound chicken tenders, cut into ¾-inch pieces
1 cup coarsely chopped onion
1 can (about 15 ounces) Great Northern beans, rinsed and drained
1 can (about 15 ounces) black beans, rinsed and drained
1 can (about 14 ounces) Mexican-style stewed tomatoes
2 tablespoons Texas-style chili powder seasoning mix
Hot cooked rice (optional)

1. Spray large saucepan with cooking spray; heat over medium heat. Add chicken and onion; cook and stir over medium to medium-high heat 5 to 8 minutes or until chicken is browned.

2. Stir remaining ingredients into saucepan; bring to a boil. Reduce heat to low; simmer, uncovered, 10 minutes. Serve over rice and garnish, if desired. *Makes 6 (1-cup) servings*

Noodle Soup Parmigiano

3 cups water
½ pound boneless skinless chicken breasts, cut into
  ½-inch pieces
1 cup chopped fresh tomatoes *or* 1 can (8 ounces) whole peeled
  tomatoes, undrained and chopped
1 pouch LIPTON® Soup Secrets Noodle Soup Mix with Real Chicken
  Broth
½ teaspoon LAWRY'S® Garlic Powder with Parsley (optional)
½ cup shredded mozzarella cheese (about 2 ounces)
  Grated Parmesan cheese (optional)

In medium saucepan, combine all ingredients except cheeses; bring to a boil. Reduce heat and simmer uncovered, stirring occasionally, 5 minutes or until chicken is cooked through. To serve, spoon into bowls; sprinkle with cheeses. *Makes about 5 (1-cup) servings*

Black and White Chili

Chicken & White Bean Stew

1 tablespoon BERTOLLI® Olive Oil
2 medium carrots, sliced (about 2 cups)
1 medium onion, thinly sliced
2 cloves garlic, finely chopped
1 tablespoon balsamic vinegar
1 pound boneless, skinless chicken breasts or thighs, cut into chunks
1 jar (1 pound 10 ounces) RAGÚ® Old World Style® Pasta Sauce
2 cans (15 ounces each) cannellini or white kidney beans, rinsed and drained
  Pinch crushed red pepper flakes (optional)

In 12-inch skillet, heat oil over medium heat and cook carrots, onion and garlic, stirring occasionally, 5 minutes or until vegetables are tender. Stir in vinegar and cook 1 minute. Remove vegetables.

In same skillet, thoroughly brown chicken over medium-high heat. Return vegetables to skillet. Stir in Pasta Sauce, beans and red pepper flakes. Bring to a boil over high heat. Reduce heat to medium and simmer covered, stirring occasionally, 15 minutes or until chicken is no longer pink. Garnish, if desired, with fresh parsley and serve with toasted Italian bread. *Makes 6 servings*

Pantry Soup

2 teaspoons olive oil
8 ounces boneless skinless chicken, cubed
2 cans (14.5 ounces each) CONTADINA® Diced Tomatoes with Italian
    Herbs, undrained
¾ cup chicken broth
¾ cup water
1 cup canned garbanzo beans, undrained
1 cup canned kidney beans, undrained
1 package (16 ounces) frozen mixed vegetables
½ cup dry pasta (rotini or rotelle), cooked and drained
2 teaspoons lemon juice
    Optional condiments: grated Parmesan cheese, chopped fresh
    basil or parsley, croutons

1. Heat oil in 5-quart saucepan with lid; sauté chicken about 3 to
4 minutes or until cooked, stirring occasionally.

2. Mix in tomatoes, broth, water, garbanzo and kidney beans; cover
and bring to a boil. Add mixed vegetables and pasta; bring to a boil.

3. Reduce heat; cover and simmer 3 minutes or until vegetables are
tender. Stir in lemon juice; serve with condiments, if desired.

Makes 6 to 8 servings

Mexicali Chicken Stew

1 package (about 1¼ ounces) taco seasoning mix, divided
¾ pound boneless skinless chicken thighs, cut into 1-inch pieces
    Nonstick cooking spray
2 cans (about 14 ounces each) stewed tomatoes with onions, celery
    and green peppers
1 package (10 ounces) frozen corn
1 package (9 ounces) frozen green beans
4 cups tortilla chips

1. Place half of taco seasoning in small bowl. Add chicken pieces; toss to coat with seasoning.

2. Coat large nonstick skillet with cooking spray. Cook and stir chicken 5 minutes over medium heat.

3. Add tomatoes, corn, beans and remaining taco seasoning; bring to a boil.

4. Reduce heat to medium-low; simmer 10 minutes. Top with tortilla chips before serving.   *Makes 4 servings*

Serving Suggestion: Serve nachos with this tasty stew. Spread tortilla chips on a microwavable plate; dot with salsa and sprinkle with cheese. Heat in a microwave oven just until the cheese is melted.

Prep and Cook Time: 20 minutes

tip *To make this flavorful stew even lower in fat, simply substitute boneless skinless chicken breasts for the thighs, and top with baked tortilla chips.*

Mexicali Chicken Stew

82

Hearty Chicken and Rice Soup

10 cups chicken broth
 1 medium onion, chopped
 1 cup sliced celery
 1 cup sliced carrots
 ¼ cup snipped fresh parsley
 ½ teaspoon cracked black pepper
 ½ teaspoon dried thyme
 1 bay leaf
1½ cups chicken cubes (about ¾ pound)
 2 cups cooked rice
 2 tablespoons lime juice
   Lime slices for garnish

Combine broth, onion, celery, carrots, parsley, pepper, thyme and bay leaf in Dutch oven. Bring to a boil; stir once or twice. Reduce heat; simmer, uncovered, 10 to 15 minutes. Add chicken; simmer, uncovered, 5 to 10 minutes or until chicken is cooked through. Remove and discard bay leaf. Stir in rice and lime juice just before serving. Garnish with lime slices. *Makes 8 servings*

*Favorite recipe from **USA Rice Federation***

tip *For quick cracked black pepper, use a mortar and pestle. If you don't have a mortar and pestle, you can use two heavy skillets (not nonstick). Place the peppercorns inside one skillet and press down on them with the other skillet to crush them.*

Hearty Chicken and Rice Soup

Brunswick Stew

2 pounds chicken pieces
2⅓ cups cold water, divided
1 can (about 14 ounces) whole tomatoes, cut up and undrained
2 large stalks celery, sliced
1 medium onion, chopped
2 cloves garlic, minced
1 bay leaf
½ teaspoon salt
⅛ teaspoon ground red pepper
6 small unpeeled new potatoes (about ¾ pound), cut in half
1 cup frozen succotash (about ½ of 10-ounce package)
1 cup cubed ham
1 tablespoon all-purpose flour

1. Combine chicken, 2 cups cold water, tomatoes with juice, celery, onion, garlic, bay leaf, salt and red pepper in 5-quart Dutch oven. Bring to a boil over high heat. Reduce heat to medium-low; simmer, uncovered, 45 minutes or until chicken is tender, skimming foam that rises to top.

2. Remove chicken from broth and let cool slightly. Discard bay leaf. Skim fat from soup.

3. Remove chicken meat from bones; discard skin and bones. Cut chicken into bite-size pieces.

4. Add potatoes, succotash and ham to Dutch oven. Bring to a boil. Reduce heat; simmer, uncovered, 20 minutes or until potatoes are tender. Stir in chicken.

5. Stir flour into remaining ⅓ cup cold water until smooth. Stir into stew. Cook and gently stir over medium heat until bubbly.

Makes 6 servings

Brunswick Stew

Chicken Gumbo

2 tablespoons all-purpose flour
2 teaspoons blackened seasoning mix or Creole seasoning mix
¾ pound boneless skinless chicken thighs, cut into ¾-inch pieces
2 teaspoons olive oil
1 large onion, coarsely chopped
½ cup sliced celery
2 teaspoons minced garlic
1 can (about 14 ounces) fat-free reduced-sodium chicken broth
1 can (about 14 ounces) stewed tomatoes
1 large green bell pepper, cut into pieces
1 teaspoon filé powder (optional)
2 cups hot cooked white rice
2 tablespoons chopped fresh parsley

1. Combine flour and blackened seasoning mix in large resealable food storage bag. Add chicken; toss to coat. Heat oil in large deep nonstick skillet or saucepan over medium heat. Add chicken to skillet; sprinkle with any remaining flour mixture. Cook and stir 3 minutes. Add onion, celery and garlic; cook and stir 3 minutes.

2. Add chicken broth, tomatoes and bell pepper; bring to a boil. Reduce heat; cover and simmer 20 minutes or until vegetables are tender. Uncover; simmer 5 to 10 minutes or until sauce is slightly reduced. Remove from heat; stir in filé powder, if desired. Ladle into shallow bowls; top with rice and parsley.

Makes 4 (1½-cup) servings

Note: Filé powder, made from dried sassafras leaves, is used for thickening and flavoring gumbos.

Prep Time: 15 minutes
Cook Time: 40 minutes

Chicken Gumbo

Tuscan Chicken with White Beans

1 large fresh fennel bulb (about ¾ pound)
1 teaspoon olive oil
½ pound boneless skinless chicken thighs, cut into ¾-inch pieces
1 teaspoon dried rosemary
½ teaspoon black pepper
1 can (about 14 ounces) stewed tomatoes
1 can (about 14 ounces) chicken broth
1 can (16 or 19 ounces) cannellini beans, rinsed and drained
  Hot pepper sauce (optional)

1. Cut off and reserve ¼ cup chopped feathery fennel tops. Chop bulb into ½-inch pieces. Heat oil in large saucepan over medium heat. Add chopped fennel bulb; cook 5 minutes, stirring occasionally.

2. Sprinkle chicken with rosemary and pepper. Add chicken to saucepan with fennel; cook and stir 2 minutes.

3. Add tomatoes and chicken broth to saucepan; bring to a boil. Cover and simmer 10 minutes.

4. Stir in beans; simmer, uncovered, 15 minutes or until chicken is cooked through and sauce thickens. Season to taste with hot sauce, if desired. Ladle into shallow bowls; top with reserved ¼ cup chopped fennel tops. *Makes 4 servings*

Prep Time: 15 minutes
Cook Time: 35 minutes

Tuscan Chicken with White Beans

Sandwiches

& SALADS

Tangy Italian Chicken Sandwiches

2 cups chopped cooked chicken breasts or turkey breast
2 ounces reduced-fat provolone cheese slices, diced
⅓ cup drained bottled hot or mild pickled vegetables
    (giardiniera)
¼ cup chopped fresh parsley
3 tablespoons reduced-fat Italian salad dressing
¼ teaspoon dried oregano
4 rounds pita bread, cut in half crosswise
8 leaves romaine or red leaf lettuce

1. Combine chicken, cheese, vegetables, parsley, dressing and oregano in medium bowl; mix well.

2. Line each pita half with lettuce leaf. Divide chicken mixture evenly among pitas. *Makes 4 servings*

Prep Time: 15 minutes

Tangy Italian Chicken Sandwiches

Chicken and Black Bean Salad

2 tablespoons vegetable oil, divided
1 medium red onion, diced
1 pound boneless skinless chicken breasts, cut into ¾-inch pieces
1 can (16 ounces) black beans, rinsed and drained
1 medium tomato, diced
½ cup pepperoncini peppers, seeded and diced
3 tablespoons chopped fresh parsley
2 tablespoons cider vinegar
1 teaspoon salt
1 teaspoon TABASCO® brand Pepper Sauce
Lettuce leaves
Whole pickled peppers for garnish

Heat 1 tablespoon oil in 10-inch skillet over medium heat. Add red onion; cook until tender, about 5 minutes, stirring occasionally. Remove to large bowl. In same skillet, add remaining 1 tablespoon oil. Over medium-high heat, cook chicken pieces until well browned on all sides and no longer pink, about 5 minutes, stirring occasionally.

In large bowl, toss red onion with chicken, beans, tomato, diced pepperoncini peppers, parsley, vinegar, salt and TABASCO® Sauce to mix well.

To serve, line large platter with lettuce leaves; top with chicken salad. Garnish with pickled peppers, if desired. *Makes 4 servings*

Chicken and Black Bean Salad

Easy Chicken & Rice Wraps

1 (6.8-ounce) package RICE-A-RONI® Spanish Rice
2 tablespoons margarine or butter
1 (16-ounce) jar salsa*
12 ounces boneless, skinless chicken breasts, cut into thin strips
    (about 3 breasts)
1 cup canned black or red kidney beans, rinsed and drained
1 cup frozen or canned corn, drained
8 (6-inch) flour tortillas, warmed
    Shredded Cheddar cheese and sour cream (optional)

*Or, use 2 cups chopped fresh tomatoes or 1 can (about 14 ounces) tomatoes, chopped, if desired.

1. In large skillet over medium-high heat, sauté rice-vermicelli mix with margarine until vermicelli is golden brown.

2. Slowly stir in 2 cups water, salsa, chicken and Special Seasonings; bring to a boil. Reduce heat to low. Cover; simmer 15 to 20 minutes or until rice is tender and chicken is no longer pink inside.

3. Stir in beans and corn; let stand 5 minutes before serving. Serve in tortillas with cheese and sour cream, if desired.   *Makes 4 servings*

Note: To warm tortillas, wrap them in aluminum foil and bake them in a 350°F oven for about 5 minutes. Turn off the heat; leave tortillas in the oven until ready to serve.

Prep Time: 10 minutes
Cook Time: 30 minutes

Chicken Parmesan Hero Sandwiches

4 boneless, skinless chicken breasts (about 1¼ pounds)
1 egg, slightly beaten
¾ cup Italian seasoned dry bread crumbs
1 jar (26 to 28 ounces) RAGÚ® Old World Style® Pasta Sauce
1 cup shredded mozzarella cheese (about 4 ounces)
4 long Italian rolls, halved lengthwise

1. Preheat oven to 400°F. Dip chicken in egg, then bread crumbs, coating well. In 13×9-inch glass baking dish, arrange chicken. Bake, uncovered, 20 minutes.

2. Pour Pasta Sauce over chicken, then top with cheese. Bake an additional 10 minutes or until chicken is no longer pink in center. To serve, arrange chicken with sauce and cheese on rolls.

Makes 4 servings

Prep Time: 10 minutes
Cook Time: 30 minutes

Chicken Caesar Salad

¼ cup plus 1 tablespoon Caesar salad dressing, divided
6 ounces chicken tenders, cut in half lengthwise and crosswise
   Black pepper
4 cups Italian salad greens mix (romaine and radicchio)
½ cup croutons, divided
2 tablespoons grated Parmesan cheese

1. Heat 1 tablespoon salad dressing in large nonstick skillet. Add chicken; cook and stir over medium heat 3 to 4 minutes or until chicken is cooked through. Remove from skillet to cool; season with pepper.

2. Combine greens, ¼ cup croutons, remaining ¼ cup salad dressing and Parmesan cheese in serving bowl; toss to coat. Top with chicken and remaining ¼ cup croutons.

Makes 2 servings

Chicken Parmesan Hero Sandwich

Warm Curried Chicken Salad

⅔ cup olive oil vinaigrette salad dressing
¼ cup *French's®* Worcestershire Sauce
¼ cup honey
2 tablespoons *Frank's® RedHot®* Cayenne Pepper Sauce
2 teaspoons curry powder
2 cloves garlic, minced
1 pound boneless skinless chicken breasts
1 bunch watercress, trimmed and washed
2 bananas
¼ cup coarsely chopped unsalted cashew nuts
½ cup shredded coconut

1. Place dressing, Worcestershire, honey, **Frank's RedHot** Sauce, curry and garlic in blender or food processor. Cover; process until well blended. Reserve ½ cup curry mixture for salad.

2. Place chicken in large resealable plastic food storage bag. Pour remaining curry mixture over chicken. Seal bag; refrigerate 30 minutes.

3. Prepare grill. Place chicken on grid; discard marinade. Grill over medium-high coals 15 minutes or until chicken is no longer pink in center, turning often. Arrange watercress on large serving platter. Cut chicken and bananas into thin slices. Arrange over watercress. Top with cashews and coconut. Serve with reserved ½ cup curry dressing. *Makes 4 servings*

Prep Time: 15 minutes
Marinate Time: 30 minutes
Cook Time: 15 minutes

Warm Curried Chicken Salad

Chicken & Spinach Muffuletta

4 boneless skinless chicken breasts (about 1¼ pounds)
  Salt and black pepper
1 tablespoon olive oil
¼ cup pesto
¼ cup chopped green olives
¼ cup chopped pitted black olives
1 round loaf (16 ounces) Hawaiian or French bread
2 cups fresh spinach leaves, stemmed
4 ounces sliced mozzarella cheese

1. Season chicken with salt and pepper. Heat oil in large skillet over medium heat. Add chicken; cook 4 minutes on each side or until no longer pink in center. If desired, cut cooked chicken into strips before assembling sandwich.

2. Combine pesto and olives in small bowl. Cut bread horizontally in half. Spread bottom half of bread with pesto mixture. Top with spinach, chicken, cheese and top of bread. Cut into wedges.

Makes 6 servings

Serving Suggestion: Muffuletta sandwiches can be served warm or cold. To heat, simply wrap sandwich in foil. Bake in preheated oven at 375°F for 15 minutes or until cheese begins to melt.

Chicken & Spinach Muffuletta

Tandoori Chicken Breast Sandwiches with Yogurt Sauce

4 boneless skinless chicken breasts (about ¼ pound each)
1 tablespoon lemon juice
¼ cup plain nonfat yogurt
2 cloves garlic, minced
1½ teaspoons finely chopped fresh ginger
¼ teaspoon ground cardamom
¼ teaspoon ground red pepper
   Yogurt Sauce (page 105)
2 rounds whole wheat pita bread, cut into halves
½ cup grated carrot
½ cup finely shredded red cabbage
½ cup finely chopped red bell pepper

1. Lightly score chicken breasts 3 or 4 times with sharp knife. Place in medium bowl; sprinkle with lemon juice and toss to coat.

2. Combine yogurt, garlic, ginger, cardamom and ground red pepper in small bowl; add to chicken. Coat all pieces well with marinade; cover and refrigerate at least 1 hour or overnight.

3. Remove chicken from refrigerator 15 minutes before cooking. Preheat broiler. Prepare Yogurt Sauce.

4. Line broiler pan with foil. Arrange chicken on foil (do not let pieces touch) and brush with any remaining marinade. Broil 3 inches from heat about 5 to 6 minutes per side or until chicken is no longer pink in center.

5. Place 1 chicken breast in each pita half. Top with 2 tablespoons each of carrot, cabbage and bell pepper. Drizzle Yogurt Sauce over sandwiches. *Makes 4 servings*

Yogurt Sauce

½ cup plain nonfat yogurt
2 teaspoons minced red onion
1 teaspoon minced fresh cilantro
¼ teaspoon salt
¼ teaspoon ground cumin
   Dash ground red pepper

Combine all ingredients in small bowl. Cover and refrigerate until
ready to use. *Makes about ½ cup*

Lemony Good Fruit and Chicken Salad

   Grated peel of ½ SUNKIST® lemon
   Juice of 1 SUNKIST® lemon (3 tablespoons)
1½ tablespoons vegetable oil
  1 tablespoon honey
  ¼ teaspoon *each:* ground ginger and curry powder
  1 cup shredded cooked light meat chicken
  1 cup cooked orzo pasta (⅓ cup uncooked)
  2 SUNKIST® oranges, peeled and cut into bite-size pieces
  2 medium bananas, peeled and sliced
  1 red or green apple, unpeeled, cut into bite-size pieces
  1 cup seedless green or red grapes, cut into halves
  ½ cup sliced celery

In large bowl, combine lemon peel and juice, oil, honey, ginger
and curry powder. Stir in remaining ingredients; chill. Serve on salad
greens and garnish with lemon cartwheel twists or wedges and fresh
mint leaves, if desired. *Makes 6 (1-cup) servings*

Outrageous Mexican Chicken Salad

6 cups shredded lettuce
1 bag (9 ounces) tortilla chips, crushed (about 3 cups)
2 cups cubed cooked chicken
1 can (15½ ounces) kidney beans, rinsed and drained
1½ cups prepared HIDDEN VALLEY® The Original Ranch® Salad
    Dressing
½ cup (2 ounces) shredded Cheddar cheese
    Tomatoes and olives

Combine lettuce, tortilla chips, chicken, beans, dressing and cheese in
a large bowl. Garnish with tomatoes and olives.

Makes 4 to 6 servings

Indian Summer Chicken and Rice Salad

2 cups water
2 cups UNCLE BEN'S® Instant Rice
½ cup thinly sliced zucchini
½ cup thinly sliced yellow summer squash
4 boneless, skinless chicken breasts (about 1 pound)
⅔ cup creamy Italian salad dressing, divided
2 tomatoes, chopped

1. Bring water to a boil; add rice, zucchini and summer squash.
Remove from heat and let stand 5 minutes. Cool.

2. Meanwhile, brush chicken with 2 tablespoons salad dressing. Grill
or broil 20 to 25 minutes or until chicken is no longer pink in center,
turning once. Slice diagonally.

3. Combine rice mixture with remaining salad dressing. Place on
serving platter. Surround with tomatoes and top with chicken.

Makes 4 servings

Hint: For a lighter salad with less fat, use reduced-fat salad dressing.

Outrageous Mexican Chicken Salad

Chicken Parmesan Stromboli

1 pound boneless, skinless chicken breasts
½ teaspoon salt
¼ teaspoon ground black pepper
2 teaspoons olive or vegetable oil
2 cups shredded mozzarella cheese (about 8 ounces)
1 jar (28 ounces) RAGÚ® Chunky Gardenstyle Pasta Sauce, divided
2 tablespoons grated Parmesan cheese
1 tablespoon finely chopped fresh parsley
1 pound fresh or thawed frozen bread dough

Preheat oven to 400°F. Season chicken with salt and pepper. In 12-inch skillet, heat oil over medium-high heat and brown chicken. Remove chicken from skillet and let cool; pull into large shreds.

In medium bowl, combine chicken, mozzarella cheese, ½ cup Pasta Sauce, Parmesan cheese and parsley; set aside.

On greased jelly-roll pan, press dough to form 12×10-inch rectangle. Arrange chicken mixture down center of dough. Cover filling, bringing one long side into center, then overlapping with other long side; pinch seam to seal. Fold in ends and pinch to seal. Arrange on pan, seam side down. Gently press in sides to form 12×4-inch loaf. Bake 35 minutes or until dough is cooked and golden. Cut stromboli into slices. Heat remaining Pasta Sauce and serve with stromboli.

Makes 6 servings

Chicken Parmesan Stromboli

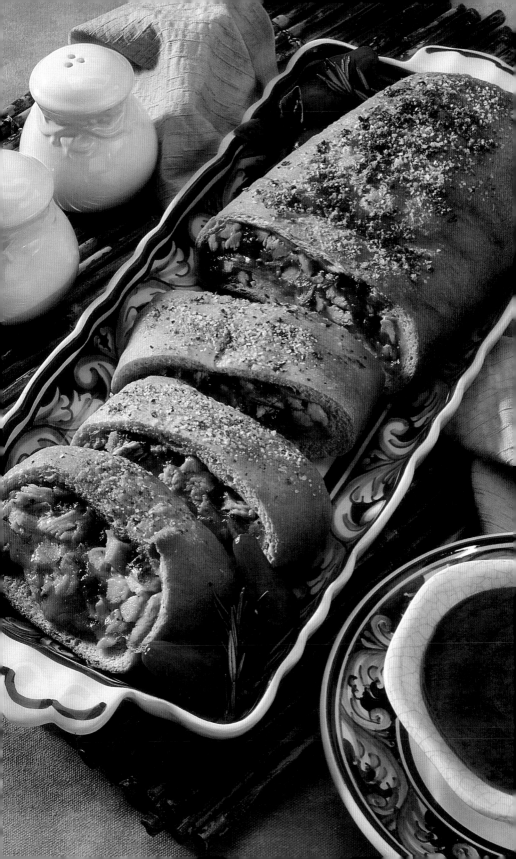

Chicken, Feta and Pepper Subs

1 pound boneless, skinless chicken breasts
3 tablespoons olive oil, divided
2 teaspoons TABASCO® brand Pepper Sauce
½ teaspoon salt
½ teaspoon ground cumin
1 red bell pepper, cut into strips
1 yellow or green bell pepper, cut into strips
½ cup crumbled feta cheese
4 (6-inch) French rolls

Cut chicken breasts into thin strips. Heat 1 tablespoon oil in 12-inch skillet over medium-high heat. Add chicken; cook until well browned on all sides and until chicken is no longer pink, stirring frequently. Stir in TABASCO® Sauce, salt and cumin. Remove mixture to medium bowl. Add remaining 2 tablespoons oil to same skillet over medium heat. Add bell peppers; cook about 5 minutes or until tender-crisp, stirring occasionally. Toss with chicken and feta cheese.

To serve, cut rolls lengthwise in half. Cover bottom halves with chicken mixture and top with remaining roll halves.   *Makes 4 servings*

tip *Choose bell peppers that are firm, crisp and heavy for their size. They should be shiny and brightly colored, and their stems should be green and firm. Store unwashed peppers in the refrigerator.*

Mandarin Chicken Salad

1 can (15½ ounces) DEL MONTE® Pineapple Chunks in Heavy Syrup, undrained
3 tablespoons vegetable oil
3 tablespoons cider vinegar
1 tablespoon soy sauce
4 cups shredded cabbage or iceberg lettuce
1 can (14½ ounces) DEL MONTE Diced Tomatoes with Garlic and Onion, drained
2 cups cubed cooked chicken
⅓ cup packed cilantro, chopped, *or* ½ cup sliced green onions

1. Drain pineapple, reserving ¼ cup syrup. In small bowl, combine reserved syrup, oil, vinegar and soy sauce; stir briskly with fork.

2. Toss cabbage with pineapple, tomatoes, chicken and cilantro in large bowl. Add dressing as desired; gently toss.

3. Sprinkle with toasted slivered almonds or toasted sesame seeds, if desired.   *Makes 4 servings*

Prep Time: 15 minutes

Mediterranean Chicken Salad

½ cup crumbled feta cheese
3 tablespoons olive oil, divided
2 tablespoons red wine vinegar
1 teaspoon sugar
¼ teaspoon salt
¼ teaspoon black pepper
1 medium onion, cut into wedges
3 boneless skinless chicken breasts (about ¾ pound), cut into strips
2 cloves garlic, minced
½ teaspoon dried oregano
3 to 4 cups salad greens
2 medium tomatoes, cut into wedges
1 cup seasoned croutons
½ cup pitted ripe olives

1. For dressing, whisk together cheese, 2 tablespoons oil, vinegar, sugar, salt and pepper in small bowl; set aside.

2. Heat remaining 1 tablespoon oil in large nonstick skillet over medium-high heat. Add onion; cook and stir 3 minutes. Add chicken, garlic and oregano; cook and stir 5 minutes or until chicken is cooked through. Remove from heat; cool slightly.

3. Arrange salad greens on 4 plates. Top with chicken mixture, tomatoes, croutons and olives. Drizzle dressing over salad.

Makes 4 servings

Mediterranean Chicken Salad

Hot Off

THE GRILL

Savory Chicken Satay

1 envelope LIPTON® RECIPE SECRETS® Onion Soup Mix
¼ cup olive or vegetable oil
2 tablespoons firmly packed brown sugar
2 tablespoons SKIPPY® Peanut Butter
1 pound boneless, skinless chicken breasts, pounded and
    cut into thin strips
12 to 16 wooden skewers, soaked in water

1. In large plastic bag, combine soup mix, oil, brown sugar and peanut butter. Add chicken and toss to coat well. Close bag and marinate in refrigerator 30 minutes.

2. Remove chicken from marinade; discard marinade. On large skewers, thread chicken, weaving back and forth.

3. Grill or broil chicken until chicken is no longer pink. Serve with your favorite dipping sauces.

Makes 12 to 16 skewers

Prep Time: 15 minutes
Marinate Time: 30 minutes
Cook Time: 8 minutes

Blue Cheese Stuffed Chicken Breasts

½ cup (2 ounces) crumbled blue cheese
2 tablespoons butter, softened, divided
¾ teaspoon dried thyme
   Salt and black pepper
4 bone-in chicken breasts (with skin)
1 tablespoon lemon juice
½ teaspoon paprika

1. Prepare grill for grilling. Combine blue cheese, 1 tablespoon butter and thyme in small bowl until blended. Season with salt and pepper.

2. Loosen skin over each breast of chicken by pushing fingers between skin and meat, taking care not to tear skin. Spread blue cheese mixture under skin; massage skin to evenly spread cheese mixture. Place chicken, skin side down, on grid over medium coals. Cover and grill 5 minutes.

3. Meanwhile, melt remaining 1 tablespoon butter; stir in lemon juice and paprika. Turn chicken; brush with lemon juice mixture. Grill 5 to 7 minutes more or until chicken is cooked through.

Makes 4 servings

Serving Suggestion: Serve with steamed new potatoes and broccoli.

Prep and Cook Time: 22 minutes

Blue Cheese Stuffed Chicken Breast

Grilled Chicken & Fresh Salsa Wraps

1 bottle (12 ounces) LAWRY'S® Herb & Garlic Marinade with Lemon
 Juice, divided
4 boneless, skinless chicken breasts (about 1 pound)
1 large tomato, chopped
1 can (4 ounces) diced mild green chiles, drained (optional)
¼ cup thinly sliced green onions
1 tablespoon red wine vinegar
1 tablespoon chopped fresh cilantro
½ teaspoon LAWRY'S® Garlic Salt
4 burrito-size *or* 8 fajita-size flour tortillas, warmed
 Salsa

In large resealable plastic food storage bag, combine 1 cup Herb &
Garlic Marinade and chicken; seal bag. Marinate in refrigerator at
least 30 minutes. In medium bowl, combine tomato, chiles, if desired,
green onions, additional ¼ cup Herb & Garlic Marinade, vinegar,
cilantro and Garlic Salt; mix well. Cover and refrigerate 30 minutes
or until chilled. Remove chicken from marinade; discard used
marinade. Grill or broil chicken until no longer pink, about 10 to
15 minutes, turning halfway through grilling time. Cut chicken into
strips. Place chicken on tortillas; spoon salsa on top and wrap to
enclose. Serve immediately. *Makes 4 or 8 servings*

Hint: This is an excellent recipe for picnics or outdoor dining. Assemble
wraps when ready to serve.

Grilled Chicken & Fresh Salsa Wrap

Buffalo Chicken Drumsticks

8 large chicken drumsticks (about 2 pounds)
3 tablespoons hot pepper sauce
1 tablespoon vegetable oil
1 clove garlic, minced
¼ cup mayonnaise
3 tablespoons sour cream
1½ tablespoons white wine vinegar
¼ teaspoon sugar
⅓ cup (about 1⅓ ounces) crumbled Roquefort or blue cheese
2 cups hickory chips
   Celery sticks

1. Place chicken in large resealable food storage bag. Combine pepper sauce, oil and garlic in small bowl; pour over chicken. Seal bag tightly; turn to coat. Marinate in refrigerator at least 1 hour or, for hotter flavor, up to 24 hours, turning occasionally.

2. For blue cheese dressing, combine mayonnaise, sour cream, vinegar and sugar in another small bowl. Stir in cheese; cover and refrigerate until serving time.

3. Prepare grill. Meanwhile, cover hickory chips with cold water; soak 20 minutes. Drain chicken; discard marinade. Drain hickory chips; sprinkle over coals. Place chicken on grid. Grill, covered, over medium-hot coals 25 to 30 minutes or until chicken is cooked through (internal temperature of 180°F), turning 3 to 4 times. Serve with blue cheese dressing and celery sticks. *Makes 4 servings*

Buffalo Chicken Drumsticks

Hot, Spicy, Tangy, Sticky Chicken

1 whole chicken (3½ to 4 pounds), cut up
1 cup cider vinegar
1 tablespoon Worcestershire sauce
1 tablespoon chili powder
1 teaspoon salt
1 teaspoon black pepper
1 teaspoon hot pepper sauce
¾ cup KC MASTERPIECE™ Original Barbecue Sauce

Place chicken in shallow glass dish or large heavy plastic bag. Combine vinegar, Worcestershire sauce, chili powder, salt, black pepper and hot pepper sauce in small bowl; pour over chicken pieces. Cover dish or seal bag. Marinate in refrigerator at least 4 hours, turning several times.

Oil hot grid to help prevent sticking. Place dark meat pieces on grill 10 minutes before white meat pieces (dark meat takes longer to cook). Grill chicken on covered grill, over medium KINGSFORD® Briquets, 30 to 45 minutes, turning once or twice. Turn and baste with KC MASTERPIECE™ Original Barbecue Sauce during last 10 minutes of grilling. Remove chicken from grill; baste with barbecue sauce. Chicken is done when meat is no longer pink near bone.

Makes 4 servings

Hot, Spicy, Tangy, Sticky Chicken

Chicken Roll-Ups

¼ cup fresh lemon juice
1 tablespoon olive oil
¼ teaspoon salt
¼ teaspoon black pepper
4 boneless skinless chicken breasts (about 1 pound)
¼ cup finely chopped fresh Italian parsley
2 tablespoons grated Parmesan cheese
2 tablespoons chopped fresh chives
1 teaspoon finely grated lemon peel
2 large cloves garlic, pressed in garlic press
16 wooden toothpicks soaked in hot water 15 minutes

1. Combine lemon juice, oil, salt and pepper in 11×7-inch baking dish. Pound chicken to ⅜-inch thickness. Place chicken in lemon mixture; turn to coat. Cover; marinate in refrigerator at least 30 minutes.

2. Prepare grill for direct cooking.

3. Combine parsley, cheese, chives, lemon peel and garlic in small bowl. Discard chicken marinade. Spread one fourth of parsley mixture over each chicken breast, leaving an inch around edges free. Starting at narrow end, roll chicken to enclose filling; secure with toothpicks.

4. Grill chicken, covered, over medium-hot coals about 2 minutes on each side or until golden brown. Transfer chicken to low or indirect heat; grill, covered, about 5 minutes or until chicken is no longer pink in center.

5. Remove toothpicks; slice each chicken breast into 4 or 5 pieces.

Makes 4 servings

Chicken Roll-Up

Jamaican Grilled Chicken

1 whole chicken (4 pounds), cut into pieces *or* 6 whole chicken legs
1 cup coarsely chopped fresh cilantro leaves and stems
½ cup *Frank's® RedHot®* Cayenne Pepper Sauce
⅓ cup vegetable oil
6 cloves garlic, coarsely chopped
¼ cup fresh lime juice (juice of 2 limes)
1 teaspoon grated lime peel
1 teaspoon ground turmeric
1 teaspoon ground allspice

1. Loosen and pull back skin from chicken pieces. Do not remove skin. Place chicken pieces in large resealable plastic food storage bag or large glass bowl.

2. Place remaining ingredients in blender or food processor. Cover; process until smooth. Reserve ⅓ cup marinade. Pour remaining marinade over chicken pieces, turning to coat evenly. Seal bag or cover bowl; refrigerate 1 hour.

3. Prepare grill. Reposition skin on chicken pieces. Place chicken on oiled grid. Grill over medium to medium-low coals 45 minutes or until chicken is no longer pink near bone and juices run clear, turning and basting often with reserved ⅓ cup marinade. (Do not baste during last 5 minutes of grilling.)   *Makes 6 servings*

Prep Time: 15 minutes
Marinate Time: 1 hour
Cook Time: 45 minutes

Jamaican Grilled Chicken

Spicy Mango Chicken

¼ cup mango nectar
¼ cup chopped fresh cilantro
2 jalapeño peppers, seeded and finely chopped
2 teaspoons vegetable oil
2 teaspoons LAWRY'S® Seasoned Salt
½ teaspoon LAWRY'S® Garlic Powder with Parsley
½ teaspoon ground cumin
4 boneless, skinless chicken breasts (about 1 pound)
Mango & Black Bean Salsa (recipe follows)

In small bowl, combine all ingredients except chicken and salsa; mix well. Brush marinade onto both sides of chicken. Grill or broil chicken 10 to 15 minutes or until no longer pink in center and juices run clear when cut, turning once and basting often with additional marinade. *Do not baste during last 5 minutes of cooking.* Discard any remaining marinade. *Makes 4 servings*

Note: Jalapeño peppers can sting and irritate the skin, so wear rubber gloves when handling peppers and do not touch your eyes.

Mango & Black Bean Salsa

1 ripe mango, peeled, seeded and chopped
1 cup canned black beans, rinsed and drained
½ cup chopped tomato
2 thinly sliced green onions
1 tablespoon chopped fresh cilantro
1½ teaspoons lime juice
1½ teaspoons red wine vinegar
½ teaspoon LAWRY'S® Seasoned Salt

In medium bowl, combine all ingredients; mix well. Let stand 30 minutes to allow flavors to blend. *Makes about 2¾ cups salsa*

Spicy Mango Chicken

Carolina-Style Barbecue Chicken

2 pounds boneless skinless chicken breasts or thighs
¾ cup packed light brown sugar, divided
¾ cup *French's*® Classic Yellow® Mustard
½ cup cider vinegar
¼ cup *Frank's*® *RedHot*® Cayenne Pepper Sauce
2 tablespoons vegetable oil
2 tablespoons *French's*® Worcestershire Sauce
½ teaspoon salt
¼ teaspoon black pepper

1. Place chicken in large resealable plastic food storage bag. Combine ½ cup brown sugar, mustard, vinegar, *Frank's RedHot* Sauce, oil, Worcestershire, salt and pepper in 4-cup measure; mix well. Pour 1 cup mustard mixture over chicken. Seal bag; marinate in refrigerator 1 hour or overnight.

2. Pour remaining mustard mixture into small saucepan. Stir in remaining ¼ cup sugar. Bring to a boil. Reduce heat; simmer 5 minutes or until sugar dissolves and mixture thickens slightly, stirring often. Reserve for serving sauce.

3. Place chicken on well-oiled grid, reserving marinade. Grill over high heat 10 to 15 minutes or until chicken is no longer pink in center, turning and basting once with marinade. *Do not baste during last 5 minutes of grilling.* Discard any remaining marinade. Serve chicken with reserved sauce.   *Makes 8 servings*

Prep Time: 15 minutes
Marinate Time: 1 hour
Cook Time: 15 minutes

Grilled Ginger Chicken with Pineapple and Coconut Rice

1 can (20 ounces) pineapple rings in juice
⅔ cup uncooked white rice
½ cup unsweetened flaked coconut
4 boneless skinless chicken breasts (about 1 pound)
1 tablespoon soy sauce
1 teaspoon ground ginger

1. Drain juice from pineapple into glass measure. Reserve 2 tablespoons juice. Add enough water to juice remaining in glass container to equal 2 cups.

2. Cook and stir rice and coconut in medium saucepan over medium heat 3 to 4 minutes or until lightly browned. Add diluted juice mixture; cover and bring to a boil. Reduce heat to low; cook 15 minutes or until rice is tender and liquid is absorbed.

3. While rice is cooking, combine chicken, reserved 2 tablespoons juice, soy sauce and ginger in medium bowl; toss well.

4. Grill or broil chicken 6 minutes; turn. Add pineapple to grill or broiler pan. Cook 6 to 8 minutes or until chicken is no longer pink in center, turning pineapple after 3 minutes.

5. Serve chicken with pineapple and rice.   *Makes 4 servings*

Prep and Cook Time: 22 minutes

Chicken Tikka (Tandoori-Style Grilled Chicken)

2 whole chickens (3 pounds each), cut up
1 pint (16 ounces) plain nonfat yogurt
½ cup *Frank's® RedHot®* Cayenne Pepper Sauce
1 tablespoon grated peeled fresh ginger
3 cloves garlic, minced
1 tablespoon paprika
1 tablespoon cumin seeds, crushed *or* 1½ teaspoons ground cumin
2 teaspoons salt
1 teaspoon ground coriander

Remove skin and visible fat from chicken pieces. Randomly poke chicken all over with tip of sharp knife. Place chicken in resealable plastic food storage bags or large glass bowl. Combine yogurt, *Frank's RedHot* Sauce, ginger, garlic, paprika, cumin, salt and coriander in small bowl; mix well. Pour over chicken pieces, turning pieces to coat evenly. Seal bags or cover bowl and marinate in refrigerator 1 hour or overnight.

Place chicken on oiled grid, reserving marinade. Grill over medium coals 45 minutes or until chicken is no longer pink near bone and juices run clear, turning and basting often with marinade. (Do not baste during last 10 minutes of cooking.) Discard any remaining marinade. Serve warm. *Makes 6 to 8 servings*

Prep Time: 15 minutes
Marinate Time: 1 hour
Cook Time: 45 minutes

Chicken Tikka (Tandoori-Style Grilled Chicken)

Lemon Pepper Chicken

⅓ cup lemon juice
¼ cup finely chopped onion
¼ cup olive oil
1 tablespoon brown sugar
1 tablespoon cracked black pepper
3 cloves garlic, minced
2 teaspoons grated lemon peel
¾ teaspoon salt
4 chicken quarters (about 2½ pounds)

1. Combine lemon juice, onion, oil, sugar, pepper, garlic, lemon peel and salt in small bowl; reserve 2 tablespoons marinade. Combine remaining marinade and chicken in large resealable food storage bag. Seal bag; knead to coat. Refrigerate at least 4 hours or overnight.

2. Remove chicken from marinade; discard marinade. Arrange chicken on microwavable plate; cover with waxed paper. Microwave on HIGH 5 minutes. Turn and rearrange chicken. Cover and microwave on HIGH 5 minutes.

3. Meanwhile, prepare grill. Transfer chicken to grill. Grill, covered, over medium-hot coals 15 to 20 minutes or until chicken is no longer pink and juices run clear, turning several times and basting with reserved marinade. (Do not baste during last 5 minutes of grilling.)

Makes 4 servings

Lemon Pepper Chicken

Quick-Fixin'

CHICKEN

Lemon Garlic Chicken & Rice

4 boneless, skinless chicken breasts (about 1 pound)
½ teaspoon paprika
⅛ teaspoon ground black pepper
2 tablespoons margarine or butter, divided
1 (6.9-ounce) package RICE-A-RONI® Chicken & Garlic
**   Flavor**
2 teaspoons lemon juice
1 medium red and/or green bell pepper, chopped

1. Sprinkle chicken with paprika and black pepper; set aside. In large skillet over medium heat, melt 1 tablespoon margarine. Add chicken; cook 2 minutes on each side. Remove from skillet; set aside.

2. In same skillet over medium heat, sauté rice-vermicelli mix with remaining 1 tablespoon margarine until vermicelli is golden brown.

3. Slowly stir in 2 cups water, lemon juice and Special Seasonings; bring to a boil. Place chicken over rice. Reduce heat to low. Cover; simmer 15 minutes.

4. Stir in bell pepper. Cover; cook 5 minutes or until rice is tender and chicken is no longer pink inside.

Makes 4 servings

Lemon Garlic Chicken & Rice

Super Speedy Chicken on Angel Hair Pasta

1 package (12 ounces) uncooked angel hair pasta
2 cups baby carrots
1 tablespoon olive oil
3 boneless skinless chicken breasts (about ¾ pound), cut into
    1-inch cubes
2 cups broccoli florets
¼ cup water
1 teaspoon chicken bouillon granules
1 jar (28 ounces) chunky-style pasta sauce
⅓ cup grated Parmesan cheese

1. Cook pasta according to package directions.

2. While pasta is cooking, cut carrots in half lengthwise.

3. Heat oil in large nonstick skillet over medium heat. Add chicken; cook and stir 5 minutes. Stir in carrots, broccoli, water and chicken bouillon. Reduce heat to low; cover and cook 5 minutes or until vegetables are crisp-tender.

4. Bring pasta sauce to a boil in medium saucepan over high heat. Place pasta on plates; top with hot pasta sauce and chicken and vegetable mixture. Sprinkle with cheese. *Makes 6 servings*

Prep and Cook Time: 25 minutes

Super Speedy Chicken
on Angel Hair Pasta

Crispy Garlic Chicken

1 envelope LIPTON® RECIPE SECRETS® Garlic Mushroom Soup Mix*
⅓ cup mayonnaise
¼ cup grated Parmesan cheese
4 boneless, skinless chicken breasts (about 1¼ pounds)
2 tablespoons plain dry bread crumbs

Also terrific with LIPTON® RECIPE SECRETS® Savory Herb with Garlic Soup Mix.

1. Preheat oven to 400°F. In medium bowl, combine soup mix, mayonnaise and cheese; set aside.

2. On baking sheet, arrange chicken. Evenly top chicken with soup mixture, then evenly sprinkle with bread crumbs.

3. Bake, uncovered, 20 minutes or until chicken is no longer pink in center.   *Makes 4 servings*

Chili Cranberry Chicken

½ cup HEINZ® Chili Sauce
½ cup whole berry cranberry sauce
2 tablespoons orange marmalade
⅛ teaspoon ground allspice
4 to 6 boneless skinless chicken breasts (about 1½ pounds)
2 teaspoons vegetable oil

Combine first 4 ingredients; set aside. In large skillet, slowly brown chicken on both sides in oil. Pour reserved chili sauce mixture over chicken. Simmer, uncovered, 8 to 10 minutes or until chicken is cooked and sauce is of desired consistency, turning and basting occasionally.
Makes 4 to 6 servings (about 1 cup sauce)

Crispy Garlic Chicken

Garden Ranch Linguine with Chicken

8 ounces linguine, cooked and drained
2 cups cooked mixed vegetables, such as broccoli, cauliflower and
    bell peppers
2 cups cubed cooked chicken
1 cup prepared HIDDEN VALLEY® The Original Ranch® Salad
    Dressing
1 tablespoon grated Parmesan cheese

Combine all ingredients except cheese in a large saucepan; toss well.
Heat through; sprinkle with cheese before serving.

Makes 4 servings

Chicken Divan

¾ pound fresh broccoli, cut into flowerets *or* 1 package (10 ounces)
    frozen broccoli flowerets
2 cups shredded cooked chicken
1 cup prepared HIDDEN VALLEY® The Original Ranch® Salad
    Dressing
1 tablespoon grated Parmesan cheese
    Cherry tomatoes

Preheat oven to 350°F. In medium saucepan, cook broccoli in boiling
water to cover until tender, about 4 minutes. Drain thoroughly; place
in shallow baking dish. Top with chicken and salad dressing. Sprinkle
with Parmesan cheese. Cover loosely with foil; bake until heated
through, about 15 minutes. Garnish with cherry tomatoes.

Makes 4 servings

Garden Ranch Linguine with Chicken

Yummy Weeknight Chicken

4 boneless skinless chicken breasts (about 1 pound), pounded thin
1 small onion, sliced
1 package (10 ounces) mushrooms, sliced
⅓ cup barbecue sauce
¼ cup honey
2 tablespoons *French's®* Worcestershire Sauce

1. Heat *1 tablespoon oil* in large nonstick skillet over medium-high heat. Cook chicken 5 minutes or until chicken is no longer pink in center. Remove chicken to serving platter; keep warm.

2. In same skillet, sauté onion and mushrooms for 5 minutes or until mushrooms are golden brown and no liquid remains. Return chicken to skillet.

3. Combine remaining ingredients. Pour into skillet. Bring to a full boil. Reduce heat and cook 2 to 3 minutes or until sauce thickens slightly, stirring occasionally. Serve with hot cooked rice, if desired.

Makes 4 servings

Prep Time: 10 minutes
Cook Time: 12 minutes

tip *To wash mushrooms, wipe them clean with a damp paper towel or rinse them briefly under cold running water, then pat dry. (Never soak mushrooms in water; they absorb water and become mushy.) Cut a small slice from the bottom of each mushroom, then slice, chop or prepare the mushrooms as directed in the recipe.*

Yummy Weeknight Chicken

No-Peek Skillet Chicken

2 tablespoons olive or vegetable oil
1 whole chicken (2½ to 3 pounds), cut into serving pieces (with or without skin)
1 can (about 14 ounces) whole peeled tomatoes, chopped
½ cup sliced fresh or drained canned mushrooms
1 clove garlic, minced
1 envelope LIPTON® RECIPE SECRETS® Onion Soup Mix*
Hot cooked noodles

Also terrific with LIPTON® RECIPE SECRETS® Savory Herb with Garlic or Beefy Onion Soup Mix.

In 12-inch skillet, heat oil over medium-high heat and brown chicken; drain. Stir in tomatoes, mushrooms and garlic combined with onion soup mix. Reduce heat to low and simmer, covered, 25 minutes or until chicken is no longer pink. Serve over hot noodles and sprinkle, if desired, with chopped fresh parsley.   *Makes about 6 servings*

Serving Suggestion: Serve with a mixed green salad and Lipton® Iced Tea.

tip *A quick and easy way to chop canned tomatoes is to cut them right in the can. Use kitchen scissors to snip them into pieces.*

Last-Minute Lemon Cutlets

2 tablespoons olive oil
1 package (about ¾ pound) PERDUE® Original Breaded Chicken
    Breast Cutlets
¾ cup white wine
2 teaspoons fresh lemon juice
2 teaspoons brown sugar
    Salt and black pepper to taste
1 to 2 tablespoons minced fresh parsley

In large skillet over medium-high heat, heat oil. Add cutlets; sauté
5 minutes or until heated through. Remove to platter and keep warm.
Reduce heat to medium. In same skillet, stir wine, lemon juice, brown
sugar, salt and pepper. Cook 1 to 2 minutes or until sauce is slightly
reduced, stirring constantly. To serve, arrange cutlets on platter;
sprinkle with parsley and spoon sauce over all. *Makes 4 servings*

Veg•All® Classic Chicken Stir-Fry

3 tablespoons soy sauce
2 teaspoons cornstarch
1 clove garlic, minced
¼ teaspoon ground ginger
1 pound boneless, skinless chicken breasts, cubed
2 tablespoons vegetable oil
1 can (15 ounces) VEG•ALL® Original Mixed Vegetables, drained
½ cup frozen broccoli flowerettes
½ cup peanuts
    Hot cooked rice

In large mixing bowl, combine soy sauce, cornstarch, garlic and ginger.
Add chicken; marinate for 20 minutes or overnight in refrigerator. In
large skillet, heat oil. Add chicken and marinade. Stir-fry chicken for
6 to 8 minutes. Add Veg•All, broccoli and peanuts. Stir-fry for 2 to
4 minutes; reduce heat and continue cooking for 2 to 3 minutes. Serve
over cooked rice. *Makes 4 servings*

Oriental Chicken & Rice

1 (6.9-ounce) package RICE-A-RONI® Chicken Flavor
2 tablespoons margarine or butter
1 pound boneless, skinless chicken breasts, cut into thin strips
¼ cup teriyaki sauce
½ teaspoon ground ginger
1 (16-ounce) package frozen Oriental-style mixed vegetables

1. In large skillet over medium heat, sauté rice-vermicelli mix with margarine until vermicelli is golden brown.

2. Slowly stir in 2 cups water, chicken, teriyaki sauce, ginger and Special Seasonings; bring to a boil. Reduce heat to low. Cover; simmer 10 minutes.

3. Stir in vegetables. Cover; simmer 5 to 10 minutes or until rice is tender and chicken is no longer pink inside. Let stand 3 minutes.

Makes 4 servings

Variation: Use pork instead of chicken and substitute ¼ cup orange juice for ¼ cup of the water.

Prep Time: 5 minutes
Cook Time: 25 minutes

Chicken with Tomato-Basil Cream Sauce

4 boneless, skinless chicken breasts (about 1¼ pounds), pounded, if desired
3 tablespoons I CAN'T BELIEVE IT'S NOT BUTTER!® Spread, divided
2 plum tomatoes, chopped
1 small onion, chopped
¼ teaspoon salt
¼ cup dry white wine or chicken broth
½ cup whipping or heavy cream
2 tablespoons loosely packed fresh basil leaves, cut in thin strips

Season chicken, if desired, with salt and ground black pepper.

In 12-inch nonstick skillet, melt 2 tablespoons I Can't Believe It's Not Butter! Spread over medium-high heat and cook chicken 8 minutes or until chicken is no longer pink, turning once. Remove chicken and set aside.

In same skillet, melt remaining 1 tablespoon I Can't Believe It's Not Butter! Spread and cook tomatoes, onion and salt, stirring occasionally, 3 minutes or until tomatoes are tender. Stir in wine and cook, stirring occasionally, 2 minutes or until wine evaporates. Stir in cream. Reduce heat to low and return chicken to skillet. Simmer, uncovered, 4 minutes or until sauce is thickened and chicken is heated through. Garnish with basil.   *Makes 4 servings*

Chicken with Tomato-Basil
Cream Sauce

The publisher would like to thank the companies and organizations listed below for the use of their recipes and photographs in this publication.

Delmarva Poultry Industry, Inc.

Del Monte Corporation

The Golden Grain Company®

Heinz North America

The Hidden Valley® Food Products Company

Hillshire Farm®

MASTERFOODS USA

McIlhenny Company (TABASCO® brand Pepper Sauce)

Perdue Farms Incorporated

Reckitt Benckiser Inc.

Unilever

USA Rice Federation™

Veg•All®

A

Apple
Apple Pecan Chicken Roll-Ups, 12
Chicken Curry, 11
Chicken Normandy Style, 34
Country Chicken Stew with Dumplings, 74
Harvest Apple Chicken & Rice, 62
Lemony Good Fruit and Chicken Salad, 105
Tomato Chutney Chicken, 66
Apple Pecan Chicken Roll-Ups, 12
Artichoke Hearts: Chicken Rustigo, 58
Asparagus
Bistro Chicken Skillet, 67
Chicken-Asparagus Casserole, 47
Avocados: Chicken Tortilla Soup, 76

B

Bacon: Southern-Style Chicken and Greens, 16
Barbecue
Barbecue Chicken with Corn Bread Topper, 28
Carolina-Style Barbecue Chicken, 130
Hot, Spicy, Tangy, Sticky Chicken, 122
Beans (*see also* **Green Beans**)
Barbecue Chicken with Corn Bread Topper, 28
Black and White Chili, 78
Chicken and Black Bean Enchiladas, 40
Chicken and Black Bean Salad, 94
Chicken & White Bean Stew, 80
Easy Chicken & Rice Wraps, 96
Mango & Black Bean Salsa, 128
Outrageous Mexican Chicken Salad, 106
Pantry Soup, 81
Tex-Mex Chicken & Rice Chili, 72
Tuscan Chicken with White Beans, 90

Bell Pepper
Barbecue Chicken with Corn Bread Topper, 28
Chicken, Feta and Pepper Subs, 110
Chicken-Asparagus Casserole, 47
Chicken Fajitas, 6
Chicken Gumbo, 88
Chicken Sauté with Olive Sauce, 52
Indian-Spiced Chicken with Wild Rice, 42
Lemon Garlic Chicken & Rice, 136
Mediterranean Skillet Chicken, 68
Simmered Tuscan Chicken, 56
Skillet Chicken Casserole, 54
Southwestern Chicken and Potato Hash, 20
Spanish Rice & Chicken Skillet, 10
Tandoori Chicken Breast Sandwiches with Yogurt Sauce, 104
Tex-Mex Chicken & Rice Chili, 72
Biscuits
Chicken & Biscuits, 4
Mini Chicken Pot Pies, 30
Bistro Chicken Skillet, 67
Black and White Chili, 78
Blue Cheese Stuffed Chicken Breasts, 116
Broccoli
Broccoli, Chicken and Rice Casserole, 26
Chicken Divan, 142
Super Speedy Chicken on Angel Hair Pasta, 138
Tomato, Basil & Broccoli Chicken, 50
Veg•All® Classic Chicken Stir-Fry, 147
Broccoli, Chicken and Rice Casserole, 26
Brunswick Stew, 86
Buffalo Chicken Drumsticks, 120

153

C
Cabbage
 Mandarin Chicken Salad, 111
 Tandoori Chicken Breast
  Sandwiches with Yogurt
  Sauce, 104
Carolina-Style Barbecue Chicken,
 130
Casseroles *(see pages 26–50) (see*
 also **Pies; Quiche)**
 Chicken & Biscuits, 4
 Chicken Divan, 142
 Classic Chicken Parmesan, 22
 Southern-Style Chicken and
  Greens, 16
Cheese
 Blue Cheese Stuffed Chicken
  Breasts, 116
 Cheesy Garlic Chicken, 38
 Chicken, Feta and Pepper Subs,
  110
 Chicken Parmesan Hero
  Sandwiches, 98
 Classic Chicken Parmesan, 22
 Monterey Chicken and Rice
  Quiche, 23
 Noodle Soup Parmigiano, 78
 Oven-Baked Chicken Parmesan,
  35
Cheesy Garlic Chicken, 38
Chicken, Cooked
 Chicken and Black Bean
  Enchiladas, 40
 Chicken-Asparagus Casserole,
  47
 Chicken Divan, 142
 Garden Ranch Linguini with
  Chicken, 142
 Lemony Good Fruit and Chicken
  Salad, 105
 Mandarin Chicken Salad, 111
 Mini Chicken Pot Pies, 30
 Outrageous Mexican Chicken
  Salad, 106
 Southwestern Chicken and
  Potato Hash, 20

Chicken, Cooked *(continued)*
 Tangy Italian Chicken
  Sandwiches, 92
 Tex-Mex Chicken & Rice Chili, 72
Chicken, Cut Up
 Bistro Chicken Skillet, 67
 Brunswick Stew, 86
 Chicken Fricassee, 19
 Chicken Puttanesca-Style, 57
 Chicken Tikka (Tandoori-Style
  Grilled Chicken), 132
 Chicken Tuscany, 32
 Country Chicken Stew with
  Dumplings, 74
 Hearty Chicken and Rice Soup, 84
 Herbed Chicken & Vegetables,
  31
 Hidden Valley® Fried Chicken, 18
 Hot, Spicy, Tangy, Sticky Chicken,
  122
 Jamaican Grilled Chicken, 126
 Lemon Pepper Chicken, 134
 No-Peek Skillet Chicken, 146
 Pantry Soup, 81
 Ranch Crispy Chicken, 10
 Southern-Style Chicken and
  Greens, 16
Chicken, Feta and Pepper Subs,
 110
Chicken, Ground: Chicken
 Normandy Style, 34
Chicken, Whole: Garlic 'n Lemon
 Roast Chicken, 24
Chicken & Biscuits, 4
Chicken and Black Bean
 Enchiladas, 40
Chicken and Black Bean Salad, 94
Chicken and Linguine in Creamy
 Tomato Sauce, 53
Chicken and Pasta Primavera, 14
Chicken & Rice Bake, 44
Chicken & Spinach Muffuletta, 102
Chicken & White Bean Stew, 80
Chicken & Wild Rice Skillet Dinner,
 56
Chicken-Asparagus Casserole, 47

Chicken Breast (*see also* **Chicken Breast, Boneless**)
Blue Cheese Stuffed Chicken Breasts, 116
Chicken & Rice Bake, 44
Crispy Baked Chicken, 14
Chicken Breast, Boneless
Apple Pecan Chicken Roll-Ups, 12
Barbecue Chicken with Corn Bread Topper, 28
Broccoli, Chicken and Rice Casserole, 26
Carolina-Style Barbecue Chicken, 130
Cheesy Garlic Chicken, 38
Chicken, Feta and Pepper Subs, 110
Chicken & Biscuits, 4
Chicken and Black Bean Salad, 94
Chicken and Linguine in Creamy Tomato Sauce, 53
Chicken and Pasta Primavera, 14
Chicken & Spinach Muffuletta, 102
Chicken & White Bean Stew, 80
Chicken & Wild Rice Skillet Dinner, 56
Chicken Curry, 11
Chicken Fajitas, 6
Chicken Parmesan Hero Sandwiches, 98
Chicken Parmesan Stromboli, 108
Chicken Rice Casserole, 41
Chicken Roll-Ups, 124
Chicken Rustigo, 58
Chicken Sauté with Olive Sauce, 52
Chicken Tortilla Soup, 76
Chicken with Tomato-Basil Cream Sauce, 150
Chili Cranberry Chicken, 140
Classic Chicken Parmesan, 22
Creamy Chicken and Pasta with Spinach, 48
Crispy Garlic Chicken, 140
Easy Chicken & Rice Wraps, 96

Chicken Breast, Boneless (*continued*)
Grilled Chicken & Fresh Salsa Wraps, 118
Grilled Ginger Chicken with Pineapple and Coconut Rice, 131
Harvest Apple Chicken & Rice, 62
Homestyle Chicken Pot Pie, 8
Indian-Spiced Chicken with Wild Rice, 42
Indian Summer Chicken and Rice Salad, 106
Last-Minute Lemon Cutlets, 147
Lemon Garlic Chicken & Rice, 136
Mediterranean Chicken Salad, 112
Mediterranean Skillet Chicken, 68
Mexican Lasagna, 36
Noodle Soup Parmigiano, 78
Orange Chicken Piccata, 64
Oriental Chicken & Rice, 148
Oven-Baked Chicken Parmesan, 35
Pizza Chicken Bake, 46
Savory Chicken Satay, 114
Simmered Tuscan Chicken, 56
Skillet Chicken Casserole, 54
Spicy Mango Chicken, 128
Super Speedy Chicken on Angel Hair Pasta, 138
Tandoori Chicken Breast Sandwiches with Yogurt Sauce, 104
Tomato, Basil & Broccoli Chicken, 50
Tomato Chutney Chicken, 66
Veg•All® Classic Chicken Stir-Fry, 147
Warm Curried Chicken Salad, 100
Yummy Weeknight Chicken, 144
Chicken Caesar Salad, 98
Chicken Curry, 11
Chicken Divan, 142
Chicken Drumsticks
Buffalo Chicken Drumsticks, 120
Spanish Rice & Chicken Skillet, 10

Chicken Fajitas, 6
Chicken Fricassee, 19
Chicken Gumbo, 88
Chicken Normandy Style, 34
Chicken Parmesan Hero
    Sandwiches, 98
Chicken Parmesan Stromboli, 108
Chicken Puttanesca-Style, 57
Chicken Rice Casserole, 41
Chicken Roll-Ups, 124
Chicken Rustigo, 58
Chicken Sauté with Olive Sauce, 52
Chicken Tenders
    Black and White Chili, 78
    Chicken Caesar Salad, 98
    Country Chicken Chowder, 70
    Monterey Chicken and Rice
        Quiche, 23
Chicken Thighs
    Barbecue Chicken with Corn
        Bread Topper, 28
    Chicken Gumbo, 88
    Coq au Vin & Pasta, 60
    Mexicali Chicken Stew, 82
    Tuscan Chicken with White
        Beans, 90
Chicken Tikka (Tandoori-Style
    Grilled Chicken), 132
Chicken Tortilla Soup, 76
Chicken Tuscany, 32
Chicken with Tomato-Basil Cream
    Sauce, 150
Chili
    Black and White Chili, 78
    Tex-Mex Chicken & Rice Chili, 72
Chili Cranberry Chicken, 140
Chutney: Tomato Chutney
    Chicken, 66
Classic Chicken Parmesan, 22
Coconut
    Grilled Ginger Chicken with
        Pineapple and Coconut Rice,
        131
    Warm Curried Chicken Salad,
        100
Coq au Vin & Pasta, 60

Corn (*see also* **Corn Bread**)
    Country Chicken Chowder,
        70
    Easy Chicken & Rice Wraps,
        96
    Mexicali Chicken Stew, 82
Corn Bread
    Barbecue Chicken with Corn
        Bread Topper, 28
    Southwestern Chicken and
        Potato Hash, 20
Country Chicken Chowder, 70
Country Chicken Stew with
    Dumplings, 74
Creamy Chicken and Pasta with
    Spinach, 48
Crispy Baked Chicken, 14
Crispy Garlic Chicken, 140
Curry
    Chicken Curry, 11
    Warm Curried Chicken Salad,
        100

D
Dumplings: Country Chicken
    Stew with Dumplings, 74

E
Easy Chicken & Rice Wraps,
    96
Enchiladas: Chicken and Black
    Bean Enchiladas, 40

F
Fajitas: Chicken Fajitas, 6
Fruit (*also see specific kinds*)
    Chili Cranberry Chicken, 140
    Grilled Ginger Chicken with
        Pineapple and Coconut Rice,
        131
    Lemony Good Fruit and Chicken
        Salad, 105
    Mandarin Chicken Salad, 111
    Orange Chicken Piccata, 64
    Warm Curried Chicken Salad,
        100

G
Garden Ranch Linguini with Chicken, 142
Garlic
Crispy Garlic Chicken, 140
Garlic 'n Lemon Roast Chicken, 24
Lemon Garlic Chicken & Rice, 136
Garlic 'n Lemon Roast Chicken, 24
Ginger: Grilled Ginger Chicken with Pineapple and Coconut Rice, 131
Green Beans
Mexicali Chicken Stew, 82
Simmered Tuscan Chicken, 56
Greens (*see also* **Cabbage; Lettuce; Spinach**)
Southern-Style Chicken and Greens, 16
Warm Curried Chicken Salad, 100
Grilled Chicken & Fresh Salsa Wraps, 118
Grilled Ginger Chicken with Pineapple and Coconut Rice, 131
Grill Recipes (*see pages 114–135*)
Indian Summer Chicken and Rice Salad, 106
Warm Curried Chicken Salad, 100
Gumbo: Chicken Gumbo, 88

H
Ham: Brunswick Stew, 86
Harvest Apple Chicken & Rice, 62
Hearty Chicken and Rice Soup, 84
Herbed Chicken & Vegetables, 31
Hidden Valley® Fried Chicken, 18
Homestyle Chicken Pot Pie, 8
Hot, Spicy, Tangy, Sticky Chicken, 122

I
Indian-Spiced Chicken with Wild Rice, 42
Indian Summer Chicken and Rice Salad, 106

J
Jamaican Grilled Chicken, 126

L
Lasagna: Mexican Lasagna, 36
Last-Minute Lemon Cutlets, 152
Lemon
Garlic 'n Lemon Roast Chicken, 24
Last-Minute Lemon Cutlets, 147
Lemon Garlic Chicken & Rice, 136
Lemon Pepper Chicken, 134
Lemony Good Fruit and Chicken Salad, 105
Lettuce
Chicken and Black Bean Salad, 94
Chicken Caesar Salad, 98
Mediterranean Chicken Salad, 112
Outrageous Mexican Chicken Salad, 106
Tangy Italian Chicken Sandwiches, 92

M
Mandarin Chicken Salad, 111
Mango
Mango & Black Bean Salsa, 128
Spicy Mango Chicken, 128
Mediterranean Chicken Salad, 112
Mediterranean Skillet Chicken, 68
Mexicali Chicken Stew, 82
Mexican Lasagna, 36
Mini Chicken Pot Pies, 30
Monterey Chicken and Rice Quiche, 23
Mushrooms
Chicken & Rice Bake, 44
Chicken Rice Casserole, 41
Chicken Rustigo, 58
Chicken Tuscany, 32
Coq au Vin & Pasta, 60
Creamy Chicken and Pasta with Spinach, 48
Harvest Apple Chicken & Rice, 62
No-Peek Skillet Chicken, 146
Pizza Chicken Bake, 46
Yummy Weeknight Chicken, 144

N
Noodle Soup Parmigiano, 78
No-Peek Skillet Chicken, 146
Nuts
  Apple Pecan Chicken Roll-Ups, 12
  Veg•All® Classic Chicken Stir-Fry, 147

O
Olives
  Chicken & Spinach Muffuletta, 102
  Chicken Puttanesca-Style, 57
  Chicken Sauté with Olive Sauce, 52
  Mediterranean Chicken Salad, 112
  Mediterranean Skillet Chicken, 68
Oriental Chicken & Rice, 148
Outrageous Mexican Chicken Salad, 106
Oven-Baked Chicken Parmesan, 35

P
Pantry Soup, 81
Parsley Dumplings, 74
Pasta & Noodles
  Bistro Chicken Skillet, 67
  Chicken and Linguine in Creamy Tomato Sauce, 53
  Chicken and Pasta Primavera, 14
  Chicken-Asparagus Casserole, 47
  Chicken Fricassee, 19
  Chicken Normandy Style, 34
  Coq au Vin & Pasta, 60
  Creamy Chicken and Pasta with Spinach, 48
  Garden Ranch Linguini with Chicken, 142
  Lemony Good Fruit and Chicken Salad, 105
  Noodle Soup Parmigiano, 78
  No-Peek Skillet Chicken, 146
  Pantry Soup, 81
  Pizza Chicken Bake, 46
  Super Speedy Chicken on Angel Hair Pasta, 138

Pies
  Homestyle Chicken Pot Pie, 8
  Mini Chicken Pot Pies, 30
Pita Bread
  Tandoori Chicken Breast Sandwiches with Yogurt Sauce, 104
  Tangy Italian Chicken Sandwiches, 92
Pizza Chicken Bake, 46
Potato
  Brunswick Stew, 86
  Chicken Tuscany, 32
  Herbed Chicken & Vegetables, 31
  Simmered Tuscan Chicken, 56
  Southwestern Chicken and Potato Hash, 20

Q
Quiche: Monterey Chicken and Rice Quiche, 23

R
Raisins: Indian-Spiced Chicken with Wild Rice, 42
Ranch Crispy Chicken, 10
Rice (see also Wild Rice)
  Apple Pecan Chicken Roll-Ups, 12
  Broccoli, Chicken and Rice Casserole, 26
  Chicken & Rice Bake, 44
  Chicken Curry, 11
  Chicken Gumbo, 88
  Chicken Rice Casserole, 41
  Chicken Sauté with Olive Sauce, 52
  Easy Chicken & Rice Wraps, 96
  Grilled Ginger Chicken with Pineapple and Coconut Rice, 131
  Harvest Apple Chicken & Rice, 62
  Hearty Chicken and Rice Soup, 84
  Indian Summer Chicken and Rice Salad, 106
  Lemon Garlic Chicken & Rice, 136
  Mediterranean Skillet Chicken, 68

Rice *(continued)*
Monterey Chicken and Rice Quiche, 23
Oriental Chicken & Rice, 148
Southern-Style Chicken and Greens, 16
Spanish Rice & Chicken Skillet, 10
Tex-Mex Chicken & Rice Chili, 72
Tomato, Basil & Broccoli Chicken, 50
Veg•All® Classic Chicken Stir-Fry, 147

S

Sausage: Chicken Rice Casserole, 41
Savory Chicken Satay, 114
Simmered Tuscan Chicken, 56
Skillet Chicken Casserole, 54
Southern-Style Chicken and Greens, 16
Southwestern Chicken and Potato Hash, 20
Spanish Rice & Chicken Skillet, 10
Spicy Mango Chicken, 128
Spinach
Chicken & Spinach Muffuletta, 102
Creamy Chicken and Pasta with Spinach, 48
Squash, Yellow: Indian Summer Chicken and Rice Salad, 106
Stir-Fry: Veg•All® Classic Chicken Stir-Fry, 147
Stromboli: Chicken Parmesan Stromboli, 108
Super Speedy Chicken on Angel Hair Pasta, 138

T

Tandoori Chicken Breast Sandwiches with Yogurt Sauce, 104
Tangy Italian Chicken Sandwiches, 92

Tex-Mex Chicken & Rice Chili, 72
Tomato, Basil & Broccoli Chicken, 50
Tomato Chutney Chicken, 66

V

Veg•All® Classic Chicken Stir-Fry, 152
Vegetables, Mixed
Brunswick Stew, 86
Chicken & Biscuits, 4
Garden Ranch Linguini with Chicken, 142
Homestyle Chicken Pot Pie, 8
Mini Chicken Pot Pies, 30
Monterey Chicken and Rice Quiche, 23
Oriental Chicken & Rice, 148
Pantry Soup, 81
Veg•All® Classic Chicken Stir-Fry, 147

W

Warm Curried Chicken Salad, 100
Wild Rice
Chicken & Wild Rice Skillet Dinner, 56
Indian-Spiced Chicken with Wild Rice, 42

Y

Yogurt
Chicken Tikka (Tandoori-Style Grilled Chicken), 132
Tandoori Chicken Breast Sandwiches with Yogurt Sauce, 104
Yogurt Sauce, 105
Yummy Weeknight Chicken, 144

Z

Zucchini
Indian Summer Chicken and Rice Salad, 106
Mediterranean Skillet Chicken, 68

159

METRIC CONVERSION CHART

VOLUME MEASUREMENTS (dry)

$1/8$ teaspoon = 0.5 mL
$1/4$ teaspoon = 1 mL
$1/2$ teaspoon = 2 mL
$3/4$ teaspoon = 4 mL
1 teaspoon = 5 mL
1 tablespoon = 15 mL
2 tablespoons = 30 mL
$1/4$ cup = 60 mL
$1/3$ cup = 75 mL
$1/2$ cup = 125 mL
$2/3$ cup = 150 mL
$3/4$ cup = 175 mL
1 cup = 250 mL
2 cups = 1 pint = 500 mL
3 cups = 750 mL
4 cups = 1 quart = 1 L

VOLUME MEASUREMENTS (fluid)

1 fluid ounce (2 tablespoons) = 30 mL
4 fluid ounces ($1/2$ cup) = 125 mL
8 fluid ounces (1 cup) = 250 mL
12 fluid ounces ($1 1/2$ cups) = 375 mL
16 fluid ounces (2 cups) = 500 mL

WEIGHTS (mass)

$1/2$ ounce = 15 g
1 ounce = 30 g
3 ounces = 90 g
4 ounces = 120 g
8 ounces = 225 g
10 ounces = 285 g
12 ounces = 360 g
16 ounces = 1 pound = 450 g

DIMENSIONS

$1/16$ inch = 2 mm
$1/8$ inch = 3 mm
$1/4$ inch = 6 mm
$1/2$ inch = 1.5 cm
$3/4$ inch = 2 cm
1 inch = 2.5 cm

OVEN TEMPERATURES

250°F = 120°C
275°F = 140°C
300°F = 150°C
325°F = 160°C
350°F = 180°C
375°F = 190°C
400°F = 200°C
425°F = 220°C
450°F = 230°C

BAKING PAN SIZES

Utensil	Size in Inches/Quarts	Metric Volume	Size in Centimeters
Baking or Cake Pan (square or rectangular)	8×8×2	2 L	20×20×5
	9×9×2	2.5 L	23×23×5
	12×8×2	3 L	30×20×5
	13×9×2	3.5 L	33×23×5
Loaf Pan	8×4×3	1.5 L	20×10×7
	9×5×3	2 L	23×13×7
Round Layer Cake Pan	8×1½	1.2 L	20×4
	9×1½	1.5 L	23×4
Pie Plate	8×1¼	750 mL	20×3
	9×1¼	1 L	23×3
Baking Dish or Casserole	1 quart	1 L	—
	1½ quart	1.5 L	—
	2 quart	2 L	—